FATHERS' BLOOD

FATHERS' BLOOD

TRUE STORIES OF PRO WRESTLING
DADS FACING THEIR GREATEST
CHALLENGER—PARENTHOOD

SEAN OLIVER

Also by the author:

Non-fiction
Kayfabe

Fiction
Sophie's Journal

Cover photo and rear photo by Mia Oliver.

ISBN: 172739190X
ISBN-13: 978-1727391909

www.seanoliverbooks.com

For Kevin, recipient of my first powerslam.

ACKNOWLEDGEMENTS

All of the interviews conducted for this book were done by the author, exclusively for this project. I'd like to thank the following participants who made time available to discuss themselves, their families, or others for me and, in turn, you: Lanny Poffo, Jason Williams, Shane Bigelow, JJ Dillon, Tito Santana, Tony Atlas, Johnny Candido, Eric Bischoff, Vince Russo, and Kevin Sullivan. Additional thanks to Eric Simms's ESS Promotions and James Soubasis at Legends of the Ring.

All family photos for this project were procured from the rightful owners for use in this book only. Official credit for each photo belongs to the individual profiled in the chapter in which the photo appears.

-S.O.

CONTENTS

FOREWORD   I

INTRODUCTION   1

1. FAMILY BEGINNINGS   15

2. WORKING PARENT   52

3. SMARTENING UP   114

4. THE SCHOOL YEARS   152

5. GOING HOME   189

ABOUT THE AUTHOR   223

FOREWORD

I have music on my mind. I sat down to read, began to do so, and it seems I've invited a haunting, of sorts. Pleasant tune—soft and melodic.

But haunting.

"They say that the road
Ain't no place to start a family"

I'm retracing my life's footsteps on the pages in my hand and learning the steps taken by others I knew in the business. I never knew them like this though, so personally. I've been given their intimate family experiences in this book, and they sit beside mine–both comparable and contrasting.

The song. I'm almost humming the damn thing now. The above lyric by Journey is from one of my favorite songs. In the 80s, it seemed to rotate regularly on the classic rock radio stations we would listen to while driving between towns when

I first arrived in WCW. It's a classic song about life on the road and the struggles of maintaining a relationship while doing the work and paying the price that our dreams require.

My own journey in the entertainment industry demanded that I was on the road often, particularly during the early part of my career. I was lucky though–I had already started my family. When I arrived in WCW and began spending time away from my wife and kids, Garett and Montanna were already 8 and 7 years old, respectively. My wife Loree and I struggled financially for so long that managing time away from family was a challenge we both were committed to manage.

And managing it was easy, in large part, because Loree is an amazing person that supported me in ways to which no words can do justice. Beyond that, my family has always been my first priority. Despite millions of miles in the air, on the road, and away from home, I averted the temptations and pitfalls that can consume a relationship. Or a life. I think I know why that was, and you'll come to know also as you read my journey beside the others profiled within *Fathers' Blood.*

My journey allowed me to include my family in much of my travel and blessed us with once-in-a-lifetime experiences that have added so much to my children's lives. I am grateful to the sports-entertainment business. I am grateful to everyone, from Verne Gagne, to Ted Turner, to Vince McMahon and everyone in between who provided opportunities that had such a profound impact on my family.

But in the pages before me, I am reminded that my family's experience in the sport was not typical. I take a moment and reflect on the pain of my brothers, pay them homage, and remind myself of all I have to be grateful for. Man, we forget sometimes.

So I will use *Fathers' Blood* to remind me to take that moment right now and do just that. I think of Garett and Montanna, along with their friend, Amy, who you will also meet in these pages. So grateful.

And most of all, I will use this book to remind me how blessed I was to know someone else.

Loree:

"Through space and time, always another show.
Wondering where I am, lost without you."

- Eric Bischoff, September 2018

INTRODUCTION

I hate myself.

I can't believe what I just did to that guy—a guy who I happen to like a lot. All for a show.

I produce interview-based programming, multiple series, multiple editions of each series, up to 18 times a year. My ideas, fleeting thoughts about what things people will find interesting, come to me in the mall, in the car, in the shower—such casual apparitions in my head. I swat 99% of them away. A few stick. Even fewer are produced, shot, and watched. It's somewhat remarkable that over the course of a few months, some random, momentarily intriguing concept is given an actual life for thousands of people. It's a really powerful thing.

It also requires responsibility, and I was feeling extremely irresponsible as I looked at a man my age, famous the world over, despair and defeat in his tearing eyes, fighting to speak over sobs. It was real. Yeah, he's a wrestler and I've seen my share of workers lean a little heavily on performance for our cameras at Kayfabe Commentaries before.

I'm a co-owner of a pro wrestling production company and we produce shows with the stars of the ring. It's reality-based, interview programming and—you may be shocked at this— those guys and gals are a little dramatic sometimes. They are performers to the core. On the whole, the wrestlers of yesterday are very engaging and have an instinctual ability to turn it on for the cameras.

However, that's not what my particular guest is doing on this night. I know him a bit, and what is happening is not a work—*fake*, in wrestling jargon. He's torn apart and I can see down to the pits of his soul. He's destroyed. Because of me. I wanted to shrink out of the host's chair and disappear.

What a great show this is, I was also thinking. Welcome to the schizophrenia that accompanies being a content producer.

I was sitting on the set of a brand new talk show we were producing called *Breaking Kayfabe.* Most of our programming to date had centered around the history of pro wrestling. Our shows featured the stars of the sport who would sit beside me and examine the details of wrestling history on-camera. Conversely, some of the series we produced covered the lighter side of the sport and our guests' colorful personalities would really unchain.

Pro wrestlers of yesteryear are like no other people on earth. I thought it would be great to produce a series that spotlighted the outside-the-ring lives and personal histories of these stars. For the most part, these people were so much more interesting than even the outlandish and over-the-top characters we'd see on TV. The wrestlers of yesteryear often led lives on the fringe, and this new series would allow us to cover all facets of these most fascinating, powerful, athletic performers, but as *people*. The tagline for the show was created– "They're people."

We would talk childhood, addiction, parenting, favorite TV shows, and anything under the sun that I saw as intriguing about these people. I wanted the actual wrestling talk kept to a minimum, unless it dovetailed into the discussion of personality and had a dramatic impact on the guest. There would be no *"Tell us about winning the championship."*

This *Breaking Kayfabe* show was certainly a risk, from a programming standpoint. The viewing public is very cynical to begin with. The *wrestling* viewing public is brutal. I could imagine the fan posts and reviews after the series pilot:

"Who the hell cares about this guy's kids?"

"When are they gonna talk about hooking up with rats?"

"I don't give a shit what his favorite cuisine is!"

Though my more pessimistic side saw some of that as a possibility, the reality was that I knew these guys and gals as people. Of course I didn't know *everything* about them, but if the tip of the iceberg was any indication of what lay beneath, then there was a ton of intriguing stuff to unearth. I was confident in that fact and also the fact that I could do it.

Getting the most guarded people in the world's most

guarded business (apart from the mob) to open up was a challenge. But it was so worth the risk of both personal failure and rejection by the viewer. I just knew if I could unveil these workers, their stories would captivate and touch viewers. The series began to feel very meaningful to me, though at the time I didn't know if it felt that way because it was just a *new* show, or a new, *important* show.

On the night in question I was sitting across from one of our first guests in the series, Sean Waltman. He wrestled as X-Pac in his more notable days and was one of the great lightweights in the wrestling game. I also found him to be a great guy, though troubled. Waltman had a past with substance abuse and his tumultuous relationship with Joanie "Chyna" Laurer was documented in the MTV series *The Surreal Life,* on TMZ, and in an unfortunate adult film. He was controversial, with baggage to spare.

Waltman was also very insightful. This wasn't a guy with a problem that walked around blaming everyone else. Sean Waltman was accountable and extremely cogent in his self-analysis. Doesn't mean he didn't have issues. He just owned them. I knew I could have a great, long-form discussion with him. Waltman was the quintessential guest for this new series which would focus on the inner lives of the wrestlers we'd known in the ring. He and I would have lots to explore. And we did.

We opened the show covering addiction, as he'd recently been arrested for a possession charge in Florida. I actually opened on the premise that I considered him a friend in the business and I would occasionally become concerned about him based on things I'd hear and read. Then that arrest hit the news. He very openly admitted to being an addict and it was a challenge. I was talking about protecting his legacy, if nothing else. He was revered in the sport. What would happen to that? But through that discussion, I didn't feel like that quite made the point in sufficiently dramatic fashion.

So I took him out at the knees.

I asked him about his responsibility to his children, who I mentioned by name. I asked what the effects of all this were on them. I think he would have rather I took out a shank and stabbed him in the gut. I basically did that, anyway.

His face went lifeless and his entire body had the air taken out of it when I mentioned his children. I said their names. I was going to beep them out anyway, but for that interview, I needed him to hear me say their names. He began to well up.

"How fucked up do you think they are, Sean?" he asked me through tears. "Pretty fucked up."

I told him there was still time to make amends. He was still alive. Reconciliation was up to him.

"I think they gave up on me, man," he sobbed. "Can you blame them?"

I tried to put some hope back in this, as I realized I'd struck a deadly artery. I wanted to walk the edge with this show, but me and Waltman fell over. I needed to infuse some optimism into the show. I don't think I succeeded in that. These were his *children* we were talking about. I'm a father. I know there is one thing that can bring any man, of any size and stature, to his knees—their child's inconsolable pain.

What had I just done?

If you watch me when he first responds to the question about his kids, I recoil. I looked down, after having started to say something in consolation, but I stopped abruptly. I wasn't sad, or emotional. I was disgusted with myself.

Had I "gone there" for the show? Was I intentionally going for an emotional response from Waltman, getting him to break down? I can't remember. All I do know for sure is that his reaction crippled me because the pain was so authentic. It was riveting. It was *real*. This was the kind of programming I envisioned for this series.

See that dichotomy? I was both disgusted as a person and excited as a producer. But I was really, really upset. I felt queasy. How could I be existing on both planes? I hated that I caused Waltman all this pain by driving my point home through the use of his children. But, as a programmer, would I have foregone that type of reality for a safer, less raw show? That attitude might be a bad compromise for the series.

Seems the choice is: being a good content producer but a lame person; or a lame content producer but a good person. Comes down to which of the two is more important to you. Not sure you can win on both counts.

Waltman's honesty and selflessness was stunning and uncommon. He bared his soul for our cameras without reservation. He wanted only the names of his children edited from the show. He said nothing of the emotional breakdown. He just wanted to protect his kids, further illustrating his desire to metaphorically throw his arms around them.

In my ten years and hundreds of interviews with professional wrestlers, I must have covered every topic under the sun. There are aspects of the sport I find interesting and talking to the makers of the magic can be a joy for both the audience and me. Viewers have a visceral experience through me, so it's important that I get the answers to the questions that they want.

Though I'm really doing the interview for the viewer, there are topics on which I will sometimes spend more time than others for my own edification. There are things I find fascinating or poignant and I hog some of the time going after those. Fortunately, those things I find interesting are usually interesting to the viewer. I say it ad nauseam—I'm first and foremost a fan of wrestling history. Therefore, my instincts will usually serve the audience. My interests usually jive with yours.

There are lots of themes that recur in our shows across all the series we produce. Who doesn't love a good rib story? The logistics of the grueling travel requirements of a marquee name in the 1980s is something to behold as well. They could have, realistically, been required to appear all across the country, for 300 of the 365 days of the year. That's fascinating to me.

I am also fascinated by blading. For the uninitiated, that is the drawing of blood at a wrestler's own hand, via the use of a sliver of razor blade slicing their forehead. That's a practice you're not likely to be asked to perform on any other job in the world.

Actually, all of the above are facets of life pretty unique to pro wrestling. I think I care far more about examining the lifestyle than the sport.

One of the recurring themes I find most interesting is the wrestling family. I've said it on camera before and it's true— I'm fascinated by what normalcy looked like in a family that had to perpetuate a lie. Did the kids know? When did they find out? What did the wife say to the moms down the block? It's all great to speculate about and even better to get actual answers to.

There was a sweetness to my mental images of the family banding together to protect kayfabe. The outside world looked at these wrestlers like gods. So too must have their own kids, right? All of our normal dads were a bit larger than life. Imagine if you watched him on TV every week hoisting giants, the crowd cheering him on. He's sweating, maybe bleeding, yelling into the mic after having won a brutal battle. *That's my dad.*

Your dad kinda sucks now, right?

But seriously, to a kid, having a dad in this business should have been the coolest thing on earth. And in some cases, I'm certain it was.

So more specific than the wrestling family, I began to see a very complex and captivating study in the lives of wrestling fathers and their children. The more wrestling fathers with whom I worked and interviewed, the more I began to see a complexity and depth to the relationships with their children.

There are clear success stories, clear failures, and a whole lot of murky water in between.

In no way are wrestlers the prototypical success stories or train wrecks as fathers. At the risk of stating the obvious, fathers in all careers and social strata run the gamut, in terms of effectiveness as parents. But there are parenting challenges unique to pro wrestling. Jesus, there are *life* challenges unique to pro wrestling. In so many ways, the lifestyle of the pro wrestler of yesteryear was unhealthy and conducive to little other than grinding out 250 dates a year, all across the country, much less raising a kid.

I keep saying *fathers* as opposed to *parents*, but there's no bias there. It just so happens that the business is 90% male. We work with mostly male wrestlers and the females that we have worked with aren't parents. Well, one actually did have a child but she has thus far kept that secret from the world.

This theme of wrestling fathers has appeared on several of our shows. Larry "The Axe" Hennig was our guest for a special called *Blood. The Hennig Wrestling Family*, wherein we explored the wrestling family and also the life and tragic death of Larry's son Curt, who wrestled most famously as Mr. Perfect. The brutish Larry "The Axe" had a quivering lip at just the mention of Curt.

We worked with manager and booker Gary Hart just a day before his passing. Since then I've had the pleasure of knowing his son Jason and I got a glimpse into the personal life of Gary and his two sons when we produced his edition of the program. I asked Jason to send us some personal photos of

Gary and the kids, out of the context of wrestling. We used the photos for the end credits of *Guest Booker with Gary Hart*. Jason's call to me the day after Gary's death was heart-wrenching. More on that later.

There are more, of course. I've chosen a handful of pro wrestlers to approach about climbing into their personal lives and their relationships with their children. I also wanted to explore a reverse perspective through the eyes of a few children of wrestlers and asked Jason Hart, Gary's son, and Shane Bigelow, son of Bam Bam, to allow me inside their lives with their dads.

I also wanted the perspective of a much younger child of a wrestler. The story people have talked to me most about from my last book, *Kayfabe,* was that of Balls Mahoney's son, Christopher. I'd see little Chris backstage at shows frequently while Balls worked in the ring. He'd occupy himself with toys while waiting, giant wrestlers wandering all around him. Then dad would be done, little Chris and Balls would head out together.

Balls died in 2016 and I think about Christopher a lot. I wanted to follow up on that story, told from the little guy's eyes. So he's in here as well, as is Balls's lifelong friend Johnny Candido, who stepped in to help with Chris in Balls's absence. Incidentally, little Chris is named after Johnny's brother Chris Candido, a former wrestler who died tragically young at 33 years-old. Balls and the Candido boys all grew up together in New Jersey.

While I wanted to update that story, I could not, in good

conscience, go into too much detail about aspects of Christopher's life today, and throughout his father's death. This was entirely my decision after researching and speaking with Johnny Candido. Chris is a young boy, with no say in what I would be writing about. He may grow up and not want a book out there depicting his grief at the loss of his dad. And it would suck if that book were out there. Would suck even more if I were the author.

So I will encapsulate the Balls Mahoney story a bit— enough to close the book on the story I started in *Kayfabe*. We can do it right here and get it out of the way:

Balls, real name Jon Rechner, was never shy about his drug use, or "medicine," as he put it. In a story I recount in my first book, one of my last conversations with him would have been sitcom laughable if he wasn't serious. Upon seeing him I commented that he looked slimmer and he said he was getting healthy, cleaning up.

"I don't drink anymore," he began, "I don't do drugs anymore, I don't to *anything* anymore. All I need are my opiates and I'm fine."

He wasn't kidding. He said they were singularly keeping him alive.

In the final months of his life, he began having a harder time getting the prescription opiates. Across the United States, particularly in states where prescription drug abuse became epidemic, authorities and lawmakers clamped down on doctors writing the scrips.

The typical, shortsighted nature of knee-jerk laws never

takes into consideration that the desperate addict doesn't just decide to quit if penalties are stiffer. And they don't just stop looking for the drug if it gets harder to find. The level of desperation rises to meet the difficulty in attainting the drug. And in these states where the prescription pads got padlocked, the street heroin ballooned in popularity again.

Suffice it to say that Balls' last few months saw very little opportunity to snag pills, where once they were a phone call away. His talk was also becoming much more fatalistic. Balls had a heart of gold, and turned his frustrations on himself. He saw his family depending on him and he knew he was coming up way short.

"I'm a burden to my family," he told a friend. "I can't walk. I can't work. I just want to check out."

After Balls died of a heart attack just after his 44th birthday, Johnny Candido kept up appearances in the Rechner home. Johnny saw his role in Chris's life as very much the stereotypical male figure. He taught Chris how to play various sports. He taught him how to ride a bike.

And also to toughen up and "be a man," as Johnny put it. If his friend Balls Mahoney's kid was going to throw a football, he was gonna do it with a tight spiral, and not look like a pussy. Johnny would help Chris become a man. It's nothing Johnny wants credit for, and he never breaks his arm patting himself on the back. He doesn't really even talk about it. It was something I uncovered while researching *Kayfabe*. Candido repeatedly tells me he's not looking for a medal. We won't give him one.

But Chris, in the face of such childhood tragedy, will never know how lucky he was that dad kept loyal friends.

I had to do a little soul-searching while writing this book. In a dilemma similar to that of the Waltman interview, I repeatedly found myself stifling the inner accusation of my being exploitative. I'm reminding myself as you read this, that I'm a producer of raw, true content. If I can't bait you with intrigue in order to bring you inside my books or KC shows, then I'm ultimately a failure at what I've set out to do. I may not change your life or make you weep, but if I don't give you something you'll always remember because it's impossible to forget, then what's it all for?

All of my research for the book was from entirely new interviews I conducted with the particular individual being profiled. The content here is new. I hate recycled matter, so this is not a paste job of stories from Kayfabe Commentaries interviews. I spoke to each of the men in this book expressly for this project, having explained only my concept for the book. Their candor is appreciated. I know you'll appreciate it as well.

Finally, there's an element of tribute to what I'm doing here with *Fathers' Blood*. That tribute extends to both the men that decided to make sacrifices in order to make a run at this sport, as well as the innocents who had those sacrifices imposed on them. Wrestling is like no other form of sport or entertainment in the world. It's neither. It's both. It's too unique to liken to anything else.

Or it was, anyway. It's important to keep sight of that fact also—wrestling today is not as it was in the eras we will be discussing. The wrestlers and the children of wrestlers with whom I've chosen to work on this project all raised children, or were raised as kids of wrestling dads, prior to the 2000s. That time seems a turning point in the business and drawing that line in the sand was necessary for me to probe the outlaw aspect of wrestling.

Outlaw daddies and their kids—that's the heart of this.

Come meet them.

1.

FAMILY BEGINNINGS

BEFORE THE WILD, mainstream success of pro wrestling in the 1980s, the sport was not exactly regarded as a wing of the entertainment business. Nor was it considered on par with traditional sport, not embodied with the glamour and sparkle of the NFL or NBA. Instead, young men with unique physiques and a willingness to embark on a lifestyle even more unique, started down the dusty roads that led to 18'x18' squares of stretched canvas.

Along that way they would partner with charlatans and castaways and mystify audiences with illusion. After an evening of sleight-of-hand, they'd then retreat back into hiding with their band of brothers. They would work this illusion in one area of the country for a time, then move on to another crop of unsuspecting fans in Territory B. They'd uproot themselves, their homes, usually a temporary set-up, and pack up the U-Haul for Destination Next.

If it sounds like a big tent circus, you're not too far off.

Wrestlers didn't get too used to the place where they laid their head. Once wrestling became national business through the advent of cable TV, they'd be dropping their head on pillows in Howard Johnsons and Holiday Inns anyway, rarely having the pleasure of the one atop their own bed.

They were always nomadic. In the early days, they hopped territories. From the 80s onward they hopped cities, crisscrossing the country as their matches played on cable TV boxes from Portland, Maine to Portland, Oregon. They saw the inside of gyms, hotels, and rental cars more than their own homes.

For a marquee name, one could be on the road for 20 or 30 days before darkening their own doorstep. Who the hell gets the mail?

As would happen with the young men on television every week, invariably some local women saw them as conquests. For those young men, new cities bore new crops of willing partners, known rather impolitely to the wrestlers, as *rats*. Some were along for the ride in a strictly sexual sense. Others fed the workers, allowed them to sleep in their places. It was a perk of the road for the boys.

Drink and drugs were not rare. A small number of the talent

kept totally clean lifestyles, while some that avoided excessive party favors for heath reasons, compromised that for steroids—seen largely as an occupational risk. This pressure to perform yielding performance enhancing assistance was not unique to pro wrestlers, as the steroid scandals in Major League Baseball, the Olympics, and other organizations have proven.

The lifestyle of the 1970s/80s pro wrestler, whether inclined to dabble in these risky behaviors or not, is atypical at best. It makes them a high risk for a young lady looking for a suitor.

On paper, you could not find a less suitable match for any woman looking for a semblance of normalcy. Some wild child looking for adventure—sure. Of course, in a young lady's heart of hearts, something more lasting would be preferred. If a solid relationship were to be the case here, it would be the women that would need to make the sacrifices, temper their fantasies, and accept a very unique reality.

For starters, even the most well-behaved, loyal, and loving wrestler would still be on the road for hundreds of days and nights a year. There were no cell phones. There was no Facetime. A pay phone call from Bennigan's to talk with the kids before they went to bed would do. If your husband said he was at a HoJo in Peoria, then you assumed that's where he was. That would have to do as well. And it would have to do for many, many nights.

Before national expansion of the sport, the demands of working a singular territory were also taxing. The blushing bride might pick the colors of the nursery and be told before the baby's birth that her man was done working Georgia, but...great news...they were ready to give him a run up in Minnesota. Call the movers, say goodbye to your mom. Might not even have to pack the backyard hammock for wintery Minneapolis.

The women must've been very much in love, and likely had balls of steel. They're the heroes.

There were also families created out of more spontaneous means. As mentioned earlier, these young, stud athletes were famous in their field and drew the attention of female fans. Couple that with the sometimes irresponsible life choices and activities that might accompany them back to the hotel rooms and, occasionally, surprising phone calls were on the horizon.

It all begs the question—just how the hell can you start to raise a family in the world of professional wrestling? Some did it well. Some did it poorly. Some tried in earnest, eventually becoming their own worst enemies. Some of the children felt a very normal existence, despite dad throwing people around on TV and being spit on. Some children saw more than they wish they had.

About the only thing that is consistent throughout all parental circumstances, all childhoods, is the baby's entry into the world.

JJ:
Lynda, Jeanette, and Lindsey

JJ DILLON WAS standing frozen, waiting for the dozen or so doctors to give off some emotional clue that things were okay, that things *would be* okay. There was a wave of conflicting emotion competing for control of his mind. Firstly, nearby lay Amanda—a gorgeous, healthy newborn brought into JJ's and Lindsey's lives about 90 minutes ago. Seeing her face was pure elation. She was the first child out of the womb and there was another one just behind. So the celebration would be truncated, as there was more happiness coming. Twins—a rare and unique joy.

The 90 minutes that would follow, though, would be harrowing. There shouldn't be more than a few minutes between the births of twins, but the little gentleman following Amanda was not coming. JJ and Lindsey didn't have much celebratory time after the arrival of their little girl because doctors made it clear the second child was to be in great crisis unless something changed.

It was an unmanageable, schizophrenic division in JJ's and Lindsey's souls. The elevation gifted by the birth of one's child is without equal. And the uncertainty of a newborn's life hanging in the balance is a helplessness that is unbearable. JJ's mind was racing, his body electrified with nervous energy. But he had to stay focused.

As each minute went by, the situation became more and more grave. Doctors came and went, assembling and repositioning around the mother—this doctor; another; that one is back; here comes another. JJ was getting very nervous. In his wrestling career he'd seen his fair share of hospitals but never had he been more unsure of an outcome. A team of dedicated physicians was working like mad to save the life of his child. Frustratingly, like a mark, all you can do is stand-by and be ready to cheer the skies above or curse the heavens like mad.

Sure, the stakes are quite different, but for a man who spent a lifetime controlling the emotions of the room, however large, this was painful.

JJ was catching snippets of conversation swirling around him in the room.

"…losing oxygen…"

"…C-section…"

He was numb. He could only imagine Lindsey's horrific frustration as she could push no harder, do nothing to save the child of her own volition. She was near collapsing from hours of trying. She could do no more. JJ could obviously do nothing. They were in purgatory.

The baby came—a boy. At the moment of birth, the doctors dove right into action. He was born totally unresponsive. The tinge of relief that came with the baby's exit from the womb was smothered with fear as doctors announced he was lifeless and rushed him to the other side of the room to begin working on him. More powder blue soldiers rushed into the room and joined the huddle on the far side, around a small table. Chaos and terror tornadoed through the room.

Time stopped for Lindsey and James Morrison.

James, known better as his on-screen persona of JJ Dillon, was 52 years-old and Lindsey was wife number three. He'd done the wife-thing and the children-thing before. But there he stood in a very different place in his very unconventional life. When you submit to a life in pro wrestling, you're already committing your days and nights to the most non-traditional career path. It would probably be unrealistic to expect the traditional family life.

JJ started out on his wrestling dream right after leaving college and the journey on the winding roads of Wonderland began. He graduated in 1964 and just two months out of college he married Lynda. He began his pursuit of becoming a pro wrestler but back then the business was so walled off. The secretive world of wrestling was so protected by gatekeepers that the road to becoming a pro could take years of dues paying. JJ found himself refereeing for eight years before getting his shot.

Conventional thinking would make most men prioritize career and stability before marriage and kids came into the picture. But nary a year after the cap and gown came the wedding coat, and in 1966 their daughter Pam was born to JJ and Lynda. Convention wouldn't be in JJ's cards in this lifetime. So referee extraordinaire JJ Dillon had a diploma, wife, and now a daughter. Why wait?

"It was the era where if you were sleeping with someone on a regular basis then you had to do the right thing and get married," he says.

As he was refereeing he found various jobs to support the new family. He taught for a while, worked as an insurance investigator for Allstate, and also had some sales jobs. He was just doing what he had to while pursuing wrestling. It wasn't happening and JJ found himself doing refereeing gigs across New Jersey and into Eastern Pennsylvania. His wrestling opportunity wouldn't come to fruition while he was with Lynda.

This marriage to Lynda lasts only four years. "I was immature and not ready for it," JJ confesses. It couldn't really be considered a fruitless false start, as it produced JJ's first child, Pam. After the split, Lynda was remarried and a stable home was built in which little Pam could grow.

A few years after that JJ was still chasing wrestling and it was time to follow the next path less beaten. Jeanette would come into JJ's life. She was five years older than the nearly 30-year-old aspiring wrestler and in marrying her, JJ acquired three stepsons, aged 9, 11, and 12. This marriage would last 17 years and would see not only the assuming of the three boys, but also the couple taking in and raising Jeanette's nieces.

It's shortly into this marriage that Ed Farhat, the original Sheik and owner of the Detroit wrestling territory, tapped JJ to come, hang up the striped shirt, and take a shot at wresting for him. He did and his career officially had some legs.

The 17 years that followed were stable in that JJ was now working as a wrestler and making a living at it.

That seventeenth year of that marriage would arrive and his time with Jeanette would come to a close. Shortly thereafter, his life would spin in yet another direction when Lindsay stepped into his world. JJ was working for WCW arranging the travel for the workers when he came across his future third bride. Lindsey was working for Amex at the time and was handling world champion Ric Flair's extensive travel from their end. Naturally, JJ's and Lindsey's work would overlap a bit since Flair was a WCW talent and when Flair recommended that Jim Crockett hire Lindsey full-time as a WCW employee, Crockett did so. She and JJ worked side by side at that point and nature took its course.

Nature also had some other truths that would impact the JJ/Lindsey union. She was 13 years younger than he. Though still in the wrestling business, the nearly 50 year-old JJ's lifestyle had settled a bit, as he was then working in the office for WCW. The madness of pro wrestling's travel demands weren't as much an issue.

"I was on the road some, but nothing like before," JJ says. "I'd go to TV every third week or go to towns that were in proximity to me."

Lindsey wanted children and being that she was in her mid-30s, she was on the clock. They'd have to start working toward this goal and their future together. JJ's schedule was certainly more in line with such a plan. But there was one not-so-minor detail that he would have to contend with if having a child were to happen—JJ's vasectomy.

Years prior, during his marriage to Jeanette, JJ had the procedure performed in Dallas. Jeanette already had the 3 boys from her previous marriage and she was 5 years older than JJ, so the question of children was moot. He'd gone in and had the procedure done in what was a 45-minute, outpatient visit. When Lindsey indicated she wanted children, JJ knew he needed a plane ticket to Dallas and an appointment at his old doctor's office.

Odds are not in the favor of one looking to reverse a vasectomy. There is an 80% chance of the *procedure's* success, and then from there one would have about a 50% chance in ever fathering a child. After a vasectomy, since the body is no longer producing sperm, it begins to shut down that process over time. After eleven years of that shut-down, simply opening up the channels mightn't work. The body has to kick back in and learn how to produce again.

The physical requirements of such a procedure are also more invasive. What began as a 45-minute doctor visit eleven years ago, would now be a 2-hour microsurgery with general anesthesia.

Lindsey badly wanted children and it would turn out to be a difficult road from her standpoint as well. After JJ's operation she would endure fertility treatments and after 2 years of that and some meds that JJ was prescribed, Lindsey was with child.

Actually, she was with children.

LANNY:
A very weak moment

MAGEN POFFO CAME into the world on May 29, 1984 to
parents Lanny and Sally, very much to the joy of both adults
and their extended families. The Poffo side of the family—
Angelo, a Catholic, and Judy, of the Jewish faith—were relieved
that Lanny had followed a traditional path. Lanny and Sally
were indeed married, and had made the conscious decision—
the right one, from Angelo's perspective—to bring a child into
the world, and a grandchild to Angelo and Judy.

The tag team of the Poffos was a formidable one. Each had
a unique style of laying it in. You probably would remember
having gone a few with either one, and both of them double-
teaming you was likely unbearable.

Yes, that tag team of Angelo and Judy Poffo could ensnare
you in a spell of Jewish guilt or Catholic rigidity that would

make you beg for a shooter's abdominal stretch. Lanny would be hooked more than a few times in his life, and on some occasions his legendarily intense older brother Randy could be thrown in for a truly impossible comeback. Lanny often seemed stuck between all three of them.

When speaking of Judy's penchant for Jewish guilt, working in the medium as expertly as Rodin sculpted, Lanny's comedy is touched with more than a hint of gravitas. It was a powerful compliment to Angelo's practice of lecturing long after his point had been made. It's a nerve-wracking cocktail:

Angelo's *"You need to…you need to…you need to…"*

Judy's *"You should have…you should have…you should have."*

Magen's new Grandpa Angelo was a professional wrestler born of Italian immigrants. Angelo wrestled from the 1950s through the 1970s and also ran the short lived International Championship Wrestling (ICW) federation out of Lexington, Kentucky in the late 70s.

They ran ICW into Tennessee, creating some opposition to the Jarretts' established Memphis wrestling territory. He promoted the renegade territory with the help of his two boys, now wrestlers themselves. Both Lanny and Randy would work for decades to come, with Lanny becoming The Genius and Randy becoming the explosively popular Randy "Macho Man" Savage.

When you were the son of a successful, traveling pro wrestler back then, there wasn't much of a choice as to your vocation. Perhaps it's no different than growing up in and around any other line of work in which your entire family was enmeshed. There's a good chance you'll pick up the reins from dad. And sometimes you did it, like it or not, son.

Lanny was working the New Brunswick, Canada loop for promoter Emile Dupree in 1983 when he and Sally were married in Canada on August 26th. He'd been with his Kentucky-bride since 1979 and living in sin with her for three years. Certainly by 1983, the tag team of Judy and Angelo were going to town on their unmarried 28-year-old son.

Maybe there was some trace of religion in their pressure on Lanny to marry Sally. More than anything though, the family was just in love with her. They made that clear. Lanny also felt the pressure from across the aisle as well.

"In a very weak moment, I succumbed to the pressure," Lanny said.

He was not anti-marriage as an establishment or a proclamation of one's love for another. He certainly wasn't disenfranchised with Sally. There wasn't an embedded case of commitment-phobia.

What there *was* inside Lanny was a rejection of, and reluctance to follow, the repeated, patriarchal dictates from above. Angelo was a powerful figure. Judy was right beside him working the guilt angle. Randy was a force to be reckoned with, even on his calmest days. The family was ready for marriage and let Lanny know it.

Wrestlers travel—a lot. Back before the sport became a national affair with the advent of cable TV, wrestlers would work a number of territories across the United States for months at a time, then move on to another one in an effort to preserve their freshness and marketability. *Florida was great to wrestle in for the past six months, but it's time to head up to North Carolina for a while. You could always come back to Florida in a year. Might make a big splash when you run back into the ring on TV for the first time in a year!*

That was the mentality in the business back then and with scant exception, workers hopped around the territories, staying alive by staying new. It made perfect business sense and that structure was really a godsend to any wrestler who could bounce around a ring a bit and talk a good game when someone shoved a mic at you. You could make a living wrestling.

You also would have to uproot yourself every six months or so. And if there was a wife at home, she was being uprooted too. Well, damnit, she signed up for that shit. Unless she'd married an accountant who decided one Tuesday morning that he was tossing the practice aside and traversing the country in a mask and tights, the ladies likely knew the deal. There was an excitement in that, too.

In this nomadic form, Lanny and Sally met in Lexington, Kentucky, were married in New Brunswick, Canada, and had a child in Shreveport, Louisiana. The considerations of the pedestrian, working crowd—*Is it the right time to have a baby, honey? Your company makes you fly to Phoenix every six months, ya know?*—was a world away from the mindset of a pro wrestler in 1983. Travel was expected. Time away from loved ones was the norm. And loading that station wagon and U-Haul every year or so was going to happen.

A wresting child of a wrestling father had seen this as a kid

29

and this *was* the norm. It was more of a challenge for the wives and mothers at home running the ranch.

Oh, but who the hell thinks about that while dancing at the wedding? It's an exciting adventure and everyone is along for the ride. No one around you thinks this is batshit. Almost all of your wedding guests are in the business.

The wedding cake wasn't even digested and the questions about having children began. Lanny was ready to make a move again, leaving Dupree's New Brunswick-based promotion and heading down to Louisiana for promoter Bill Watts. Relocating wouldn't necessarily be an impediment in planning for a family, though. This was the lifestyle.

Sure enough, Sally was soon with child and Lanny was getting mat burn for Watts's Mid-South Wrestling, working the huge Louisiana territory which, in actuality, touched into neighboring states. It was massive and made for long travels in the loop.

Playing into the unpredictability of the wrestling lifestyle, Lanny was let go from the territory when Bill Dundee was brought in as the new booker. In pro wrestling, the booker is the person charged with making the creative decisions for the company. They decide what will be happening, who will be doing it, and if you're not in their plans, you're not working.

"When Bill Dundee came in with the book," Lanny began, "I was fired immediately, along with about ten other people. Because they were bringing in new people."

With a child months from arrival, most people would come unglued at this news. They'd be on the phone with every promoter in the country, trying to line up the next gig. Poffo had something else in mind.

With Sally in her last trimester of pregnancy, Lanny decided he wouldn't uproot her. Instead, he told Bill Watts he would actually hang around Shreveport, unemployed. They were in the homestretch and they would have the baby there. Lanny just wanted to let Watts know he'd be around, if needed.

Good fortune came in the form of Tom Zenk. Well, in the form of Tom Zenk flaking-out on Bill Watts and quitting with no notice, leaving a bunch of unfilled bookings for upcoming matches. Watts got on the phone with Lanny and offered him Zenk's open dates. Poffo took the dates from Watts, now able to keep working though the birth of the baby.

Zenk was known to be temperamental and unappreciative throughout his career. Good thing for Lanny.

"Everyone gave Zenk the world and he threw it on the ground," Lanny says. "But the story of my life is: I pick up the scraps."

On May 28, 1984, Lanny took the long, all-night drive home to Shreveport from a shot in Ft. Worth, Texas. The following day Lanny found himself in the hospital, ready for the birth of his child. Sally's water had broken and now they were there waiting.

As Lanny waited with his mother-in-law, the doctor came out and told Lanny they may need to perform a C-section.

"We will give it an hour," he said. "If nothing happens we will perform the cesarean."

Lanny knew of a wrestler named El Gaucho who'd told

Lanny that his child was born with a mental handicap as a result of having been left in the womb with the umbilical cord around its neck. Lanny heard the doctor's plans to wait a while to see if the birth could happen naturally and he became nervous.

"Doctor," Lanny began, "I'm just a high school graduate but wouldn't it be better to do the C-section now in case the umbilical cord is wrapped around the baby's neck and it's not getting enough oxygen?" The doctor looked at Lanny. And replied crudely.

"Mr. *Poe-foe,*" he said, "you're right. You're a high school graduate. See this?" He pointed to a machine. "This is a fetal monitor. If the baby weren't getting enough oxygen, I would be the first to know." Lanny was too relieved to be pissed at the insult.

He thanked the doctor, who'd unknowingly avoided a front facelock.

"I'd rather take a chance and be an ass, than be sorry forever," Lanny reflected.

An hour passed with no progress. The doctor decided to go ahead with the procedure and Lanny decided to leave the room. No amount of in-ring bloodshed would prepare him for what he would have seen if he stayed.

At 7:30 p.m., Lanny Poffo became a father.

TONY:
One night with Joyce

THERE WAS A MAN waiting to meet wrestling star Tony Atlas at an NWA show in West Virginia. Well, there were lots of people—men, women, and kids—waiting to meet him. He was making waves in the sport and was a bona fide attraction.

But Norris McDuffie wasn't your average fan. Wasn't even a fan, really.

Church-going Christian folk like Beatrice and Norris McDuffie didn't accept the notion of babies born out of wedlock, certainly not in their family. They were Virginians—they walked with God and stepped with morality as they did. The South in the United States during the 1970s was still a stronghold of traditional values. The South meant religion, meant moral code. Mama and Papa raised their kids to act that way, and they set the example.

Being from the South meant something, and a smear on those values also meant something. To be the subject of scandal would result in stares in the grocery store and whispers at church. On the more severe end of things, it might mean being ostracized in the community. Could mean extended family pulling away. What was actually considered scandalous had a range, of course. In the rocking and rolling 1970s, was having a baby before marriage really a community headline?

Illegitimate—that's what you heard sometimes.

In a weird way, it also mattered on which side of the fence that illegitimacy fell. The family of the father of the child would have been seen differently than that of the mother. Your spunky young man out there doing his thing was positioned a little differently than your little girl out there, doing *anyone's* thing. Double standards and the #hashtag equality movement was decades away.

So the McDuffie folk may have had it a touch easier with a piece of news they'd just received. See, they were in a unique position in their staunch, Christian community. Their boy had become famous recently. He was on TV every week and performed all over the Carolinas and Virginia before thousands of fans.

Now, their son Tony was in a bit of a pickle and Mama Beatrice, for one, wasn't having it. Mister Big Shot would still have to work within the laws of God and congregation.

It was 1977 and Tony Atlas was now a star in the Mid-Atlantic wrestling territory, based in the Carolinas. He was a tag team champion in the mainstay NWA territory. He'd soon be on his way to the Georgia Championship Wrestling territory to replicate that success with a new tag team partner, Tommy Rich. He was a true bodybuilder who stood over six feet—a unique commodity in pro wrestling at that time. There were wrestlers with large physiques, big and muscular. But Tony was a legitimate, competitive bodybuilder, chiseled and defined beyond anything seemingly possible.

When Tony walked into the ring, it was an event. When he appeared in a close-up on the TV screen, flexing and posing, it was breathtaking. He may really have been the first black superhero.

Being in such a position puts a young man in a moral conundrum. The road was full of temptation for a popular pro wrestler. Drinking from the stream of excess was standard fare for the bruised brethren. Shit, some bathed in it.

Tony was no stranger to the practice of meeting young ladies, enamored by his celebrity and massive frame. He was quite a sight to behold and a black superstar in such physical condition was gold for promoters. Tony was in demand—both in the rings and in the bedrooms.

Tony first laid eyes on Joyce in Columbus, Georgia. She was interested. He was interested. This was par for the course and Tony had no reason to hesitate. He was a single guy, successful at his craft, and this was all part of the spoils associated with his fame. Tony slept with Joyce just one time.

Tony was out the door and back out on the road for Jim Crockett's Mid Atlantic promotion without batting an eye. At that point, there was nothing significant about the encounter.

Nothing yet known to either party, anyway.

Not long after, Joyce reached out to Tony and said she was carrying their child. What could he say? There was a fair amount of on-the-road exploits, maybe this happened to all the boys. Maybe it happened more than once, to each of the boys. Tony didn't exactly have grounds to refute it. Would he begin the line of questioning—*Was I the only guy? Couldn't it be someone else? You sure?*

But that seemed futile and Tony's upbringing took over. He'd been raised in a Christian family so he knew that the moment any discussion of having children came up, it had better be accompanied by the planning of a wedding.

But Tony was on the road so he just swallowed this information and carried it with him. There was no big discussion with the family, a grand counsel of decision makers and offers of comfort. Tony knew how Beatrice would likely feel. Norris, his father, was a more complicated matter. Tony hadn't seen his father in twelve years. They'd been apart since Tony was 12 years-old. That alone was a commentary on the responsibilities of fatherhood, and could have served as a built-in crutch for Tony to bail on Joyce and their new situation.

Beneath the monster frame, Tony was a good-hearted guy and he wanted to do the right thing by all parties involved. Tony didn't offer objection to Joyce and didn't shirk responsibility.

Norris McDuffie waited for Tony at that NWA show in West Virginia. Tony came out to see him and laid eyes on his father for the first time in half his life. There were a million things on which they could catch up. There were a million things that Tony, under normal circumstances, could have said to him. But in recent days, there was really only one thing on Tony's mind. Somehow, in the fractured discussion of an estranged father and son reunion, Tony realized he needed something more than the catching-up bullshit.

Tony needed a father.

He needed to talk to his father about his becoming a father. So right then and there, Tony and Norris, familiar strangers to each other, went on to a difficult subject. Tony told him about Joyce's pregnancy and that he was confused about next steps. Norris listened to the while predicament.

"Do you love her?" Norris asked. It was an impossible question.

"I don't know," Tony said. "I don't even hardly know her name." Could he learn to love her? Should he? Crapshoot, all around.

After breaking the ice speaking to Norris about this, Tony knew he needed to get Beatrice up to speed. She was no-nonsense, and his counseling session with Beatrice was much simpler than his with Norris.

"Don't say you don't love that woman," she began, "because you sure loved her that night." The implications in the shadow of the crucifix would be huge for Beatrice and the family, had Tony not done the right thing. She was coming from a place of religion's hard and fast rules. And a little tough-love thrown in the mix.

"You don't want your child to be a bastard," she told Tony.

The people closest to him had weighed in. For his father, it seemed a question of love. For his mother, it was about doing the right thing, finishing the thing he started one night some months ago in Columbus, Georgia.

Tony's one night stand was a gamble that so many of the wrestlers of the era risked countless times.

From it was born a young lady, by all accounts lovely. Could you really call it a mistake? What was unplanned and unexpected does not necessarily mar the existence of said, whether it be a child or anything else. Tony and Joyce had a chance encounter that gave life—a life that grandchildren are now thankful for as well. An entire chain of life is set off by solitary events, affecting so many.

Who are we, who am *I,* to have almost branded the pregnancy born of the one night stand in Columbus as a pitfall of the road? Upon reflection it's safe to say that the percentages are greatly stacked against any couple forging a happy, nuclear home for children born of one night encounters. However it doesn't mean those kids born to strangers drawn to a night of passion will be any less happy. That kind of thing is determined by decisions those parents make when it comes time to let the baby fever fade, and take a good, long look across the room to that person with whom they partnered.

Tony's indecision and desire for counsel on the question of marriage was complicated by the absence of his father, Norris. It seemed that norm would set a template. But for the meantime, with a baby on the way, marriage was a norm dictated by Tony's mother, as well as his Lord.

We saw that same Lord pretty prominent in the decision for marriage in another wrestler, as Lanny Poffo served Lord and family just as Tony did. In Lanny's case there was no baby on the way when the question of marriage was raised. Yet the call of doing the right thing, as instilled by upbringing, guided both Tony and Lanny in their individual situations. Something larger was at work—overbearing parents and overbearing Gods make things happen.

We've seen the most amount of family planning on the part of JJ Dillon, spanning nearly 30 years, and including the reversal of a vasectomy. JJ was thrice married and they all ran their course with time. In that respect, JJ is unique in the profile here.

But Tony Atlas's planning of wife and child, not necessarily in that order, was the most spontaneous in our examples. Regardless of the precipitating events, Tony decided to buckle down and do what all seemed to consider the right thing.

Tony asked Joyce to marry him. Joyce, originally from Alabama, then moved to Georgia with Tony to begin their life together and prepare for the birth of their child.

A precious, little lady named Nikki was on her way into Tony Atlas's life. But things wouldn't stay sunny for long.

TITO:
What the good Lord wants

ONE NICE THING about working for Verne Gagne's AWA in the early 80's was the company's plane. It turned overnight shots into day trips. The prospect of workers being back home on the same night they wrestled 300 miles away was a lifesaver for guys with wives and children.

Tito Santana had neither a wife nor child when entering pro wrestling by way of pro football, having been drafted by the NFL's Kansas City Chiefs and then playing Canadian football. The young athlete of Mexican descent would eventually find his way into the squared circle after football died out, having been cut after one season in Canada. While playing college football for West Texas State, his team was quarterbacked by future wrestler Tully Blanchard. Incidentally, an inordinate number of pro wrestlers would pass through the college. Must've been offered as a major.

Tito headed to the Florida wrestling territory where he was trained by Japanese star Hiro Matsuda. He stepped into a ring for the first time in 1977 in Florida.

Within a couple of years, Tito did a stint in New York, cutting his teeth in a big city before heading to the AWA's home base of Minnesota. Tito worked for Vincent J. McMahon's WWWF in 1979-1980 and then headed to Minnesota for Verne Gagne's hardscrabble territory. He put in a couple of years for Verne, and the AWA's fairly regular schedule made it a stable territory in which to work and settle down a bit.

Merced, Tito's real name, married the very strong and independent Leah when he was 28 years-old. It took a special lady to accept the transient lifestyle and uncertainty that wrestling offered. And if the marriage was to go the distance, there had to be both great effort on the part of the wrestler, and also a disposition most rare on the part of the wife.

Tito didn't much worry about Leah adapting to the uncertainty of the pro wrestling lifestyle, as she was a free spirit in her own right. Leah was from New Jersey, where she met Tito, but was living in Hawaii while Tito was working Verne's Minnesota-based territory. While Tito was trying to get the wrestling thing going in the mainland, she was in Hawaii working three jobs to pay the bills. She knew the importance of working hard for her family and it was often at the cost of convenience.

Eventually Leah moved to Minnesota to join up with Tito.

Though his schedule in the AWA was fairly regular—having the airplane ensured Tito would be home most nights—he'd return home quite late. If Leah was working during the day, she wouldn't see him at all, as he'd be on his way to the plane to fly out to the next city in the afternoon. This prompted Tito to ask a difficult request of Leah. Their schedule necessitated change if the marriage was ever going to be a normal husband and wife thing. Work ethic is great and all, but Leah and Merced were finding themselves married to jobs, not each other.

He eventually asked Leah if she would mind not working. A couple of days a month he'd be on a tour that required an overnighter or two. But for the most part, he and Leah would be able to have a somewhat normal schedule and see each other. Tito would be home in the daytime, and if she was also, everything would work better. Leah was a go-getter—Tito knew it was asking a lot.

Children, and the decision to have them, were not really a focal point. Tito was doing well and they were both in their late 20s. They left it up to fate. They took no precautions against having children, though.

"If the Good Lord wanted to give us a baby, we were ready for it," Tito said.

Well, the Good Lord would deliver to Leah and Tito 3 boys over the 5 years that followed. And the first one was on its way when Tito announced to a very pregnant Leah that they were heading east to Georgia where a man named Ole just made Tito some big promises.

ERIC:
The purest form of marketing

EARLY SUNDAYS WERE for wrestling. Eric and his girlfriend Loree, now well-pregnant with the couple's first child, just sat down for an early afternoon lunch. Nothing special, some imitation crab legs. They were even stained pinkish orange to look like the genuine article. They weren't that good, but that's what the budget would allow. The afternoon menu was fake crab meat and cheap champagne. Loree, being pregnant, didn't get a sip.

Money was tight and a baby was on the way. How the hell did Eric Bischoff and his girl, both former models once working and living in Chicago, end up here? Winters in central Minnesota were not for the weak. The Braham, Minnesota farm house in which they sat watching Verne Gagne's pro wrestling product had one source of heat—a wood burning stove in the basement. Winter nights were frequently falling below zero and that meant getting up in the middle of the night and throwing more firewood into the stove.

It sounds rough and it was. They'd left modeling back in Chicago when they realized that it was less a life of glamour than it was a life of uncertainty. Eric was bouncing in a bar and Loree was a cocktail waitress. They'd met in Minneapolis and followed the lure of the big city.

But enough was enough. The reality of the modeling world became apparent and they were smart enough to see the signals. The big city buck was tough to come by and the dashing couple dashed off to Minneapolis again.

In short order they found themselves way up in Braham, about sixty miles north of Minneapolis, when Eric landed a spot as a regional sales manager for an agricultural equipment company. He was particularly amused by the looks of the locals when he and Loree would go into town for breakfast. Loree was 23 years-old in early 1984 but she looked around 15 years-old. She would head into the rural diner with a bump on her belly and a grown man on her arm. Creep alarms went off all over the place when the townies saw the little girl with that slickster.

So there they were, freezing their asses off in central Minnesota with not much more than each other. They may not have had a lot, but Eric had one important thing.

Salesmanship.

Sales was nothing new to Eric—before modeling he'd been a sales manager for a food processing company in Minneapolis.

He had the gift of gab, an electric smile, and a kind of charm with which one might talk themselves into a closed sale or a successful bank robbery. So young Mr. Bischoff kept at it, doing the grind in the frigid northern Midwest.

How prophetic when the future president of a $300 million dollar entertainment entity, then eating imitation crabmeat, pointed to the TV and said to his girl Loree, "That is the purest form of marketing, right there." He was pointing to Verne Gagne's AWA product—pro wrestling. Yeah, he liked it as a kid, still watched it on Sundays. But it was nowhere on his radar as anything other than casual entertainment.

Loree would have their baby, a youngster named Garett. Eric would officially make Loree 'Mrs. Bischoff' just five months after Garett came into the world. Montanna, Garett's younger sister, would join everyone just a year later.

This family formation, an Americana story born out of love and hard work, would go a few more years before becoming a wrestling story. And it wouldn't be a wrestling story that could sufficiently feed the Bischoff family for several years after that.

But one day in 1987, little Garett, then three years-old, bid farewell to his dad who was headed out of the house for a rather spontaneous business meeting with Mr. Verne Gagne— that guy he'd seen on TV countless times on his Sunday wrestling program. Eric Bischoff would meet Verne as well as Mike Shields, a gentleman running the business operations at the AWA, and soon this family story would morph into a wrestling family story.

VINCE:
Top salesperson

WHAT WAS THERE FOR Vince and Amy to really talk about this time? They would be on child number three, with two boys already bouncing around their new Connecticut home. V.J. and Will, 6 and 9 years-old, would be getting a sister in the coming months. The Russo clan was about to grow, as were Vince's responsibilities in the company for which he worked.

Vince and Amy had landed in a comfortable place in the mid-1990s after rocky times, uncertainty their guide. The hardworking, blue-collar guy with the entrepreneurial streak had just lost his video rental stores in Coram and Lake Ronkonkoma on Long Island, NY. An opportunity to work for World Wrestling Entertainment was a blessing and, good Lord, money, money, money.

It wasn't a lot of money at that point, but it was not tied to the sale of a new TV set or washing machine. After his video stores went belly up, Vince got a job at a local P.C. Richard & Sons appliance store. Never one to grow moss and seemingly always finding himself selling something anyway—new video tape rental, TV set, himself—the job made sense and paid the bills.

More than that, it delivered some stability to Amy and the family. In time, Vince became the top salesperson at that Long Island location. Easy to believe. If you've talked to Vince Russo for about two minutes you soon realize he's slipped the fatigues on your body, placed the musket in your hand, and already began walking you toward the battlefield as you chatted. Well, he chatted. You nodded and tried to keep up.

Shit, wrestling was cool, too. He watched it as a kid, entertained by the Vince J. McMahon product and the in-ring salesmanship of Chief Jay Strongbow, Gorilla Monsoon, and Bruno. Plus it was finally an opportunity to make good on the promise of that college degree in journalism. He'd be writing. There was a stint back in '85 at Harper and Row Publishing, but that was just something right out of college. Now, someone wanted to pay him to write. Ultimately, to run a real publication—one that his dad could grab at a news stand.

Putting aside the debate of "real publication," the fact remained that he'd be writing for a big company, and for a steady paycheck. He didn't walk into WWE offices as a fan. The product had been entertaining years ago, sure. But he needed a job. P.C. Richard wasn't where he saw himself.

Annie, the third Russo child, was born in 1995 in the warmth of that steady WWE gig. Russo had done a lot to secure his employment with Vince K. McMahon, revamping the company's magazine and making it a real sales tool for the company's core product. Russo put himself on the road with the product. The previous editor of WWE Magazine compiled the product entirely from the offices. Distancing the magazine from the talent to that degree necessitated the fabrication of all its content. It didn't sit well with Russo when he took the reins.

"I thought that was ridiculous because they had access to all the talent," Russo says. "Why would you make the stuff up?" He put himself on the road beside WWE talent at the TV tapings and did the interviews there. He concocted story ideas for the magazine from watching what was going on. Finally, the magazine was moving in tandem with what was being produced for TV.

The schedule put Russo out of the home for a few days a week, which wasn't all that bad. Bringing little Annie into the fold wouldn't be an issue. Amy was on board.

"She knew my schedule," he said. "She knew I was on the road." If they had a pay-per-view show that weekend, Russo would fly out on Saturday and fly back into town on Tuesday. For regular TV weeks he wouldn't have to leave until Sunday and he'd be back Tuesday or Wednesday. He was only gone half the week.

Though, that didn't mean his responsibilities for WWE were finished when that plane touched down. Not by a long shot. And soon, after the family settled in, Russo would be handed a responsibility that would pull him much further away from V.J., Will, Annie, and Amy.

If Russo seemed a little directionless in the first stanza of his adult life, he wouldn't be alone. In the beginning, with his first wife Lynda, JJ Dillon was a knock-around guy with jobs in insurance and sales. He was young, married, and soon a parent to Pam. Success in wrestling was years away, in a strikingly similar template to that of Eric Bischoff and also Vince Russo. The main difference in them was their plans for wrestling—JJ's dream of doing more than the refereeing he was doing, and both Vince's and Eric's absence of a dream of wrestling superstardom.

But those guys all found the sport that would deliver them, some time after settling down with a wife and having a child. It's worth noting that all those men list sales as a career before wrestling, and all men became noted for talking on camera or writing for it, rather than beating anyone up. Wrestling—yes Eric, in its purest form—is all about the pitch. One guy did it beside the biggest heel faction of the 1980s, another guy did it beside the biggest heel faction of the 1990s, while the other was writing for the biggest babyface faction of the 1990s.

Different styles, different looks, different eras, but they all had that same intangible that makes you want to listen, and makes bosses want them in the office.

How 'bout that? A few sales guys, skilled talkers, bouncing around trying to light a fire. And what is sales, at its core?

I spent time in real estate and I remember a quote from a high-priced sales course that sounded as much like justification for date rape as for accepting the fact that you were in sales.

"I'm not convincing anyone to buy anything. I'm just helping them realize they want to do something they had no idea they wanted to."

Should it be no surprise that there is a sales background in three of the men that would become integral to the creative offices in the two major pro wrestling federations? A lot of knock-around cats find themselves in sales because they've been hustling their entire lives. The circus tent calls to the runaways. And back then, the wrestling business was loaded with guys looking for something to keep them tethered to the earth.

Guys on the fringe—that's the glamorized image of a wrestling federation in the 70s and 80s, before MTV embraced it. A renegade soul, a little directionless but avoiding jail for the moment, could find a home in pro wrestling. Brothers all of them, who all knew something we didn't. The business was well-suited to one with a vagabond spirit.

But not necessarily to children. As for the wives of guys working in the ring, well they knew what they were signing up for. The kids were the unwitting participants in a life less typical. They would endure the pains of endless travel too, alongside mom and dad. Bloody images of dad showing up on magazines and on television are not the norm for a school-age kid. Those kids at school are talking too, saying that dad is a fake. Could be tough to navigate.

Or was it?

2.

WORKING PARENT

TODAY'S WORKPLACE REALITY offers generous
paternity time off, up to two weeks in the U.S., for the father of
the newborn child. It might be inconceivable for younger
people to imagine a time where workplaces offered no pay for a
day not worked. Through broken bones, sprained muscles, and
births, the wrestler showed up to be manhandled in a ring that
night, hundreds or thousands of miles away, or there was no
pay for the day.

Wrestlers have long been considered independent
contractors—that designation generating much head-scratching
given the requirements and restrictions placed upon them by
singular corporations for whom they exclusively perform.

Without belaboring a point not relevant to our topic, in the United States a worker is either designated as an employee or an independent contractor. Each carries with it certain rules and regulations that must be met by the employer in order for such designations to be upheld.

Designating one a full-time employee requires the employer to make available certain benefits to the worker. There are the obvious, like health care packages, protections from workplace harassment, and the like. More subtle are things like sick days, and personal days off. Consider the toll offering pro wrestlers the option of taking a sick day on an evening for which they were advertised in a Heavyweight Title cage match would take on a federation. Offers a little perspective on wrestling companies fighting to classify wrestlers as independent contractors instead.

The most sacred of human experiences, the birth of one's child, will likely mean a day away from the ring for the pro wrestling dad. With any luck, the wife holds out until an off day or well after midnight if her husband is wrestling in their home state.

If there's barely time to gaze into the face of your newborn baby before you're headed back out on the road, then it stands to reason that time at home in the child's formative years will be scant as well. There will be soccer games, school events, parents' nights, and all that.

But formal events aside, what of first words, first steps, bad grades, fights at home, fights at school? There is just nothing built into the wrestling world to accommodate for these moments. But no one is surprised. It's what everyone signed up for.

Well, everyone but the kid.

JASON:
We came first

THE RATHER TERRIFYING, bald-headed, heel manager Gary Hart stood with the thick leather belt dangling from one hand.

"One now...or two later?" he asked. He began to slowly wind the strap, which he diabolically dubbed Sweet Lucy, around his hand. He waited patiently for the answer before serving up the punishment.

Viewers all over Dallas, Charlotte, and Atlanta saw this man's sideways and vicious actions unleashed upon their heroes every week on TV. This day, however, saw no television cameras around Gary. There was no audience. There was only Gary and Jason, his young son.

The little bugger messed up again. And damnit, he had to make the choice—one whack now, or two later?

Jason didn't have to think very hard on that one. He knew he should always take the strap right then and there. That decision was not rooted in the economics of *one now, two later*. Most kids would have gladly agreed to two shots at a later time just to get the big, imposing figure in the doorway to turn and leave. Maybe they could change his mind during the stay of execution—make dad a sandwich, bring him a beer.

No. Jason knew himself and brother Chad well enough to know time would not be on his side. Putting off Sweet Lucy only gave him and his brother more time to fuck up again, and then there would surely be a little more mustard in the swings to come.

Jason would take the one whack now and forego the anticipation.

In a flash it was done. Gary was off, back downstairs to the den, hoping enough of a lasting impression was made to make his kid a damn man someday. Gary often made it known that there were specific character traits expected of his boys. He greatly valued honesty and integrity. He would tell Jason and Chad many times that there was nothing worse than a liar and a thief. Tough love was sometimes the way to go when his kids got sideways with those principles.

Gary Williams, his identity when not wielding belts and shadowing vicious, on-camera heels, was not necessarily a church-going man but he believed in the Christian principles and imparted them to his boys. He lived by them himself. But when things went wrong, particularly later on after a few tarnished report cards, Jason would see some of the Gary Hart that we all knew.

At some point in the day, after Sweet Lucy's justice, Jason would eventually amble his sore ass downstairs and pass by dad.

"Hey sport," Gary called out as he walked by. It was over. Punishment served, lesson hopefully learned. Back to life.

Jason's memories of dad are many. Indeed wrestling dads did the road and were gone for long stretches, but Gary's time at home was sacred to both he and the boys. Just how much time he had at home would vary. When Gary was working the Dallas territory for promoter Fritz Von Erich, he could get home five nights out of the week. It seemed he was always home, at times to the great chagrin of Jason The Mischievous. The Dallas years were a bad time to try and get away with shit.

"When he was working for Fritz in Dallas and he was home a lot, I couldn't get over with much," Jason said. "I wasn't like Bing Crosby's kids or anything. There were rules I had to follow."

In Jason's 5th grade year in the summer of 1988, the family moved out to Daytona Beach. Uncle Kevin (Sullivan) hooked up Gary with a nice place out in the Florida sun. Gary went back to work and this time he was in WCW, a national operation with far greater reach than World Class Championship Wrestling out of Dallas.

Prior to 1988 when Gary first hit the Charlotte territory, later to become WCW, it was run by Jimmy Crockett and travel would have Gary on the road for spurts, nothing consistent. He might be out doing cities for eleven days, home for maybe four days. Then back out. In that structure, a wrestler could still have a sense of normalcy with their family. They would be with them for a stretch, then gone for a bit. Back then under Crockett, it was still a regional territory operation, hitting a few neighboring states, and seeing some limited expansion to big cities like Chicago and Philadelphia. But for the most part, Gary could get home for eight days or so, per month.

By 1988 and Gary's return to WCW—the new, national WCW—things had changed. Media mogul Ted Turner had bought WCW, and the operation grew quickly. The guys were handed stacks of place tickets, literally. When Gary left the his home, plane tickets in hand, he would not return for six-week periods. That was an absence unlike any others Jason and Chad had to endure prior.

But despite the extended time away, when Gary was home, he made it count. He loved the business, for sure. But he loved home as well. They were two separate things—both important, both passions.

"When he was home, he was *home*," Jason said. He is quick to point out that Ric Flair's declarations on an ESPN documentary of not being able to stand it when home, and counting the minutes until the road again pulled him out the door, were not how Gary lived his life. When he was working for WCW and he'd get a few days home after a weeks long jaunt around the country, he'd actually get a little mopey the day before heading back out for another few weeks on the road.

"Well, at least I get to see my friend Steve Williams tomorrow," he'd say as he shuffled around the house, searching for the consolation. "Get to see my friend Hawk, too." There was something sacred about time at home with the family.

That made for some real memorable time with dad. Looking back now, Jason sees how affirming that was. But, truth be told, back then when dad was home it cramped the young metalhead's style more than a little. They were breaks in the six-week runs of hell raising.

Before Gary's national WCW run, the Dallas territory days saw Gary on the homestead much more often and present in their lives. Makes it tough to get away with shit if you're a young man filled with, er, adventurous energy and Gary Hart is always a few hours from walking in that door every night.

But now that dad was gone for six-week stretches with Turner's WCW, Jason's leash didn't just lengthen—it fell off.

Lost in the sounds of Motley Crue's *Decade of Decadence* compilation and the ubiquitous Guns n' Roses *Use Your Illusion* releases, the 15 year-old Jason would really test the boundaries. Jason was finding himself in more and more trouble. One night Jason's mom was on her nightly phone call with Gary, who was calling in from the road. She listed some events that their youth-gone-wild was perpetuating and that list went on a bit too long for everyone's liking. Gary listened.

"I'll be home Wednesday," was all Gary said.

Goddamn, talk about an effective promo. It was always the most loquacious guys that got credit for being the best on the mic. Seems that promo effectively left so much to the horrifying limits of the imagination that Gary could have shortened his on-camera promos by about 1,000 words.

Jason ruminated on that declaration—*He'll be home Wednesday.*

Well, just what in the hell did that mean? Wednesday could really run the gamut on the good day/bad day scale.

Jason spent Wednesday at school, very aware that the remainder of that day would be something to contend with. Around 3:00 on the prescribed day, Jason came out of school and his heart skipped a beat. There it was, right outside school—the car. Dad was back home, and dad was *there*. Each step Jason took toward the car felt like it was more uphill than the last.

What would happen when he opened the door? All those kids around him were still dismissing. Maybe it was better that he came to pick him up from school rather than Jason walking into the lion's den at home. Couldn't kill him out here. Too many witnesses.

Jason slipped into the back seat which would soon be rendered either a confessional or a carving station, depending on Gary's level of disappointment.

Gary looked at Jason in the rearview mirror and put his fingers beside his mouth, contemplatively. He'd done this many times in the televised promos. But this was the real deal. He spoke soft and even.

"Son," he started. "I don't have that much time with you. I don't wanna spend it disciplining you. So please— *straighten...up.*" He just stared at him in the mirror. Jason waited. There was nothing more. Nothing but the stare. Jason nodded.

That resonated. Gary had framed it just right. Their time together was always limited. Did Jason really want to lose sight of the clock by aggravating his dad?

"I wasn't the class clown," Jason began, "but I was his writer. I flocked to the kids that were the disciplinary problems."

In his teen years, his grades began to fall. Jason was becoming distracted by the metal scene, trying on some rebellion for fashion, and flexing a little more attitude. What worked for Vince Neil or Axl Rose didn't necessarily translate to the 16-year-old listening to the music. Rebellion is easy from the comfort of your million dollar mansion in Los Angeles, which did not have Gary Hart roaming around wrapping a belt that he gave a goddamn name to, around his fist.

As Jason's issues with high school grades continued, Gary and WCW parted ways. He was home now. With wrestling out of his life and no income to keep the family afloat, things weren't rosy for him either. His deteriorating finances were beginning to take a toll on both him and the family. The marriage was on the rocks. He was on edge.

Jason's rock star rebellion made regular appearances at school. There were calls to the Williams home from the school. Report card day was the formal proclamation that Jason was not a frontman in *G n' R* or *Crue*, but perhaps the frontman in a band of his own creation, called The Fuckups. As and Bs on the report card became Fs and when Jason displayed little concern, Gary lit up. Seeing Jason's failure topping the collection of Gary's mounting troubles made him see red.

Gary made a bee-line for his son, grabbed him, and drove him backwards. He pinned Jason against the wall and leaned in, nose to nose. Gary's voice spoke quietly while his eyes, locked on Jason's, screamed.

"I know I lost all my money, I got no career no more, and I know your mother's gonna leave me...but you *will* respect me." He searched his son's eyes. "You may not respect anyone else, but you're gonna respect *me.*"

Change soon came. Jason took responsibility for his life.

"I straightened up after that," he said. "I always had the guitar and rock 'n roll thing. But I always knew I was loved. There were limits. It's effective parenting."

There were times Gary resorted to using Dusty Rhodes as an unwitting accomplice in keeping Jason in line. Dusty was running the show as booker for WCW at the time. After Jason's more recent issues in school, Gary made it knows that if ever he went back to wrestling full-time, Jason was being sent to military school. When things would get sketchy at home, Gary would walk out of the room saying simply, "That's it, I'm calling Virgil and goin' back." Virgil was Dusty's real name and Gary's return to WCW would mean a uniform, crew cut, and boot camp mornings for Jason.

Jason came home from school the day after one such proclamation.

"Dad, did you call Dusty?" he asked timidly.

"I certainly did. He said Jim Herd was gone and I can come back whenever I want. And I'm goin!" He threatened it for months and months. He never went back.

Gary walked out on his wrestling career and a six-figure salary with even more on the table for a future commitment. Taking himself off the road caused great personal struggles as well as financial.

Gary and wife Twinkle never divorced but were separated a number of times over the years. She was never really a wrestling wife, in the most typical sense. She was friends with a couple of the wives, notably Austin Idol's wife and One Man Gang's wife. She did like some of the guys, particularly Dick Murdoch, Michael Hayes, and Al Perez. But Twinkle stayed away from the matches. She went to a big Texas Stadium show and a Cotton Bowl show, but that was about it. Gary's work world was his own.

Their longest and final separation lasted ten years. Jason, noting how much time they'd spent apart, asked his dad why they didn't just divorce already.

"Cause I'm not paying for another fucking thing," Gary said.

LANNY:
Different than Angelo

ANGELO POFFO'S SHADOW started at his feet in the ring, draped across the mat, out through the ropes, and across son Lanny's life, and into Magen's nursery. Looming large in the life of Lanny, now a wrestling dad, was the wrestling dad that raised both he and Macho Man. Lessons learned from their father were, for Lanny, lessons on what *not* to do, as a father.

"I decided to raise my daughter differently than Angelo raised me," Lanny said. Despite that proclamation, much of Angelo's lifestyle was admirable, and Lanny noted that. Angelo didn't abuse alcohol or drugs. He didn't abuse the kids. Lanny's objections were more centered around Angelo's rejection of individuality. True to a promoter's mindset, Angelo would tell you to do something he wanted you to, for the sake of business. Then he'd try and *make* you something he wanted you to be, even if you were his son.

Lanny always saw himself a little left of center. And for that, Lanny was made to feel wrong.

"A lion never learns to fly and a violet never becomes a rose," he said. "You don't try and become anyone." Lanny's square peg identity was being shoved into a round hole by Angelo, and it left some emotional bruising.

Angelo, while physical in the ring, didn't ever lay his hands on Lanny. He didn't need to. Angelo's power came in other forms, not the least of which was a power from the heavens above—another form of Angelo's control that Lanny rejected.

Angelo was a devout Catholic. The rigidity of the religion's rules and the consequences of shortcomings was embedded in Lanny from a young age. The attempted embedding of Catholicism in Lanny's psyche would have recurring effects in Lanny's life, underscoring how important his father made religion.

Angelo and his bible made a rather unforgettable appearance during Lanny's first sexual experience, in a metaphoric sense. In what should have been a nearly uncontrollable moment, Lanny's tag partner below was not being compliant.

"The first time I got laid I was 16 years-old,"he confesses. "I had erectile dysfunction and it wasn't because I was old. It was because I thought I was going to hell." Lanny's pathway up the young lady's thighs became the highway to eternal damnation. This humiliation was his first step on a path of resentment.

"This whole Catholic dogma is quite bullshit," he says.

Angelo's wishes for Magen to be raised Catholic were made

known. The promoter, the boss, the father, had spoken. Lanny, of course, knew the position he was in—consistently between the wishes of the three most present people in his young life. Would this control now extend beyond just him, to fatherhood and the raising of his first and only child? It was an important crossroads for Lanny.

But Lord, if anything were important enough to make Lanny break from the influences of the elder Poffos, wouldn't it be a child? *His* child? He'd decided that he alone, along with Sally, would chart Magen's course. Angelo, Judy, Randy, and Jesus, possibly in that exact order, would need to step off this locomotive.

Individuality was going to be key in the raising of a young lady who came to the world via Shreveport, Louisiana and the Watts Mid-South territory.

She would be raised to "do her best and forget the rest," and reminded "don't let your individuality be trampled by mobs." Even today, Lanny, often conveying his thoughts in bursts of refrigerator magnet wisdom, constructs a word-borne framework in which he lives. But unlike most, Lanny actually reflects on the colloquialisms he espouses, studying their words and absorbing the message. Lanny believes what he says, whatever he is saying. And he says a lot.

After Magen's birth, Lanny was right back on the road for promoter Bill Watts in the Louisiana territory. The area serviced by Mid-South Wrestling was huge. Though based in Louisiana, it actually ran cards regularly in Oklahoma, Mississippi, and parts of southeast Texas. The territory was known for its massive span and grueling travel for its workers.

The demands didn't afford Lanny much opportunity to be around Magen and her Sally. It was the life he'd chosen, and as a Poffo, the only life he'd known. Plus, with the new face at home, it was all the more reason to trudge out and provide. Lanny, for all his stances on independence, was still old-school in many ways. He was a traditionalist. He had to bring home the bacon.

Lanny would make it a point to be present for the key moments in Magen's young life. He really felt he didn't miss much. In those early days and months, his mother-in-law was with Sally in Shreveport and meeting all the needs of the new mom. Lanny was at peace with it all. The road warrior was back out on the highways and byways, firmly ensconced in his role of breadwinner. And perhaps, finally, unchained.

TONY:
No farmer

TONY ATLAS WAS ON his way to Alabama to do great bodily harm to a man. By this time in the late 70s, Tony had logged thousands and thousands of miles doing just that—traveling to other states and battling men. He was massive, with remarkable strength.

But this was part of no angle. This would be a run-in to remember. The man in question had made the mistake of putting his hands on Nikki, Tony's little girl. She was old enough to talk now and in the spirit of the great wrestlers Tony had known, his daughter's mouth was about to start a big feud.

Some years before this, Tony had gone through with the wedding to Joyce. There was enough pressure to do the right thing and get married so that's exactly what the couple did. Tony was optimistic—he was doubling down on a long shot, having nothing to do with Tony, Joyce, or their individual personalities.

For all of Tony's effort to do what was right in the eyes of God, mom, and whoever else was weighing in on it, the core of the marriage was weak. They'd made a lifelong commitment based on the emotions of a single night. As a model, the *one-night-stand-turned-pregnancy-turned-marriage* was, in its construction, a structure erected on a Jello foundation. For something like that to succeed, it would have required the two parties spend a lot of time working on getting to know each other, while simultaneously raising a baby. A whole lot of luck would also be needed to have this seemingly random pair, having hooked up for a fling, turn out to be compatible.

Then there was Tony's job. If the above task seemed not Herculean enough to make succeed, it would have to be attempted with Tony working a full road schedule.

Did the business, in and of itself, fuck up relationships? Maybe not. But in the face of a difficult situation, one needing lots of careful attention, the pro wrestling business was not an ally.

Tony was living in Atlanta and working Jim Crockett's Mid-Atlantic territory, while Joyce was still out in Alabama. She packed up and moved to Georgia to start her new life with Tony. It was a seat-of-the-pants life thus far, and likely not easy for Joyce.

But the baby was coming. The precious, innocent life, unencumbered by anything but the need to be loved and cared for, was coming. A love like that could outlast anything.

Hyperfocused on the baby, they would make it work. They would do it for little Nikki. A child's love could galvanize even this.

This magical process would begin with the birth, of course. And right there, at the starting line, cracks already began to form. Tony was doing shows all over the Carolinas and Virginia and simply had to be on the road. Joyce was well-pregnant and found herself alone 90% of her days and nights.

Herein lies the hazy line that the business draws—where do the requirements of the job overtake moral obligation? If one took a moment to examine the NBA, NHL, NFL, or any other three letters that mean "professional athlete," they'd see a schedule with gaps, off-seasons, and home games for half the season. No other sport had the audacity to require its stars to keep the schedule and lifestyle that pro wrestling did.

Due to the lengths of his absences, Joyce, sitting pregnant and alone, elected to head home to Alabama to have the baby.

Why stay in Georgia? Joyce spent six days a week alone in their Atlanta apartment. She had come out to Atlanta knowing no one but Tony, and he was on the road six days a week. After a short time, she began going home for stretches of time. She'd become lonely and didn't want to stay. In an effort to keep Joyce in Atlanta and build a somewhat stable home, eventually her sister headed out and stayed with her to help deal with Tony's absences.

"You cannot tell a promoter in the 70s, that you're having a baby," Tony says. "They don't give a shit. They've got you booked." Promoters had you advertised and tickets were sold based on your being a part of the show. They handed you a booking sheet with your dates and cities outlined for that whole month. The Crocketts, the territory promoters, weren't open to hearing suggested changes to that schedule, from the rank and file.

That living arrangement might seem strange to someone with a more traditional existence than that of a pro wrestler of the 1970s. But Tony was working atop the tag team division at the time and he was booked solid. Tony's road schedule was so demanding that he was really only home one day a week. It didn't matter if Joyce lived in Atlanta, Alabama, or Alaska. The amount of time she'd see Tony was negligible.

Now factor the raising of a child into this. Tony's wrestling schedule saw him come home Sunday night and spend only Monday with Joyce and Nikki. He was barely seeing his wife and child and Joyce, frustrated by this, would continually return to her hometown in Alabama with the baby. Tony would return to an empty home. Struggling for some normalcy in the situation, Tony kept bringing her back to Atlanta. It felt hopeless. He stood between the business that made him a star and a good living, and his little girl, his flesh and blood.

Tony felt there was only one way their marriage would have worked—if he quit wrestling. And that just wasn't going to happen.

They tried Atlanta yet again. As a testament to how hard Tony was working on the road, he'd saved up $100,000. Joyce saw the compromise of the road schedule would be slightly more palatable if they used that money buy a house and she could go back to school. There were no roots in Atlanta, so here was a way to set up some of their own.

Tony announced he was headed to work New York—Vince J. McMahon's WWWF. He didn't want to set up roots in Atlanta—New York might pay off. Once again, despite efforts, the business flattened whatever hope they'd managed to conjure up. Joyce was not going to globe-trot and decided, desperate for some roots in her new, transient existence, left for her Alabama hometown yet again.

She didn't slam the door entirely on Tony—she'd offer one more shot for a life with her and Nikki. She told him the marriage could work only if he'd come out to Alabama with her and Nikki and become a farmer. And that was as far as she was bending, having bent again and again for Tony and pro wrestling.

"Look," Tony told her, "if you leave one more time, I'm not going to get you no more."

She did. He didn't.

Just a short time later, Tony got a phone call from an attorney. He told Tony that he was representing Joyce in the matter of her divorce and had papers with his name on them. The shrewd shark used Tony's obligations to his wrestling promotion against him.

"You got two choices," he advised the wrestler. "You can sign the divorce papers as they are and be done, or you can start disputing things and we will take you to court."

And what exactly did court mean to a professional wrestler in the 70s or 80s? Tony knew precisely what it meant, but in case he was foggy on the implications, the lawyer made it patently clear.

"You can't miss court dates or we will have you locked up, and we know that you have to go back on the road again for work."

They had him. He could have asked for certain custody arrangements with Nikki. He could have had input in the financial ramifications of the divorce settlement and payments. But that meant him getting his own attorney and, more difficult still, court dates for which he'd have to appear in person.

Tony still struggled with the idea of having a child in the world outside marriage. It bothered him. Sure, it wasn't much of a marriage so far. What kind of family life had his little girl seen thus far? What kid deserved a Monday afternoon daddy? Philosophically it was pretty clear—Tony was setting up to be an absentee everything.

He would ask around his locker room, looking for advice and an answer to how he could make a marriage to a stranger work, just so he could continue to look into the eyes of his daughter.

"If your wife wants to go," said his partner Tommy Rich, "let her go."

Tony did just that. Joyce and little Nikki made Alabama their home without Tony.

Joyce was soon involved with another man. One day Tony was told by Nikki that the man spanked her, and that brought Tony out to Alabama. He was headed right for the man's throat.

"Back then I had a temper and I had a very, very short fuse," he said. "I would have broke him in half."

Tony didn't get that opportunity. Police interceded and told him he couldn't come back. To guarantee enforcement of that, there was soon an order of protection issued. Pro wrestling had built a fence around Joyce and Nikki for Tony. Then the legal system padlocked it.

Tony had seen his daughter up to 5 years-old, then briefly again at 11 years-old. The next time his eyes would meet hers she would be married with kids of her own.

SHANE:
Dad's home

IT WAS ANOTHER LATE night in the Newark Airport terminal. Little Shane Bigelow could barely keep his eyes open but the excitement was keeping him up. The clock above their seats blinked 2:30 a.m. At just 5 years-old, he didn't know whether or not it was unusual to make trips to the airport in the dead of night to greet daddy's return flight from Malaysia, after a six-week absence. Those trips felt like forever to Shane.

But Daddy would be home now. For about two-weeks, anyway. Then he was off to Japan again. Then Korea. That would eat up another month or so.

But there were always the precious couple of weeks here and there, when dad was home. He made it count. Bam Bam Bigelow cherished the home time and would get back there as often as he could. Whenever there was a free day on the old

WWE schedule, he'd make sure he hit home. These Asia tours were tough, though. He'd be booked for a month and a half with no real opportunity to get home.

For Shane, the "Dad's home!" moments were golden, though. When Bam Bam had a break and could swing home, he would fish with Shane. They'd golf. He would drive him to baseball practice and if actual games coincided with days that Bam Bam was around, he wouldn't miss one. He made his being home an event. The times were so cool—like fishing trips that lasted 16 hours and saw Shane deposited at the school doorstep right after the outing—that Shane never saw his dad's absences as difficult. He'd find himself with mom at Newark Airport soon enough.

Plus, those toys from Japan were like nothing he'd seen here, and Bam Bam always brought some back from his tours there.

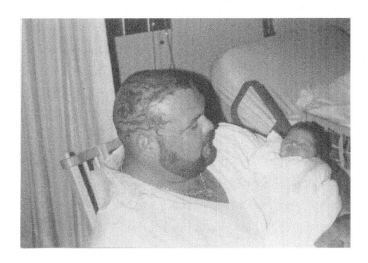

Bam Bam was a scene. For starters, he looked like a circus character and maybe that's why kids always took so well to him. There he stood at Shane's school, ready to pick him up. Within a few minutes, some little guy was scaling Bigelow's back. Another boy began climbing his right side. Bam Bam squatted to give the boy a shot at getting up and in a second he was sitting on the wrestler's shoulder. Within minutes he was a living jungle gym, and it happened a lot.

He loved it. Kids loved climbing all over his 6'4", 400 lb. frame. How often could a kid get an opportunity to see a real-life gentle giant? Much less one with flames tattooed all over his bald dome. Shane loved when all the kids would run to his dad. It made him proud that he was so loved.

Shane was used to his dad's celebrity and it really had nothing to do with the ring or the schoolyard. Scott Bigelow, Bam Bam's real name, was a local legend around town. All across Neptune and Asbury Park, NJ, it seemed everyone knew Bigelow and everyone had a story, usually outlandish. It almost became competitive to try and "out-Bam" someone else's story. He was walking folklore, with tales ranging from his flipping a police car at age 17, to his having killed a guy in a bar fight. The latter made its way up to Bayonne, NJ, where I'd actually heard it about fifteen years ago.

Beyond the campfire tales, Bigelow was a legitimate athletic wonder. He was ranked 3rd in the state of New Jersey for high school wrestling in his junior year. Even years later in pro wrestling, Bam Bam always made a show of his athleticism and agility, while working as a big man. Bam Bam threw dropkicks.

He did cartwheels—yes, literally cartwheels, in the ring. He was on his way to being one of high school's celebrated sports stars. Big things could have been in store had he not gotten thrown out of school as a senior.

As cool as all that was, Shane cared more about the fact that Bam Bam didn't miss his baseball games when he was around. The wrestling thing was great, but even better was the dad thing. And Bam Bam was good at it. He made it to recitals for his daughter and wrestling meets for his son. He made it for all the major holidays.

In Shane's early memories, Bam Bam is always there—patiently helping with homework, spending time and being the larger than life presence kids worship their dads for being. When you ask him about the absences, Shane barely recalls them. Those memories were supplanted by the other stuff. Road absences aside, and maybe even under consideration, you really couldn't ask for a dad who was more supportive, gentle, and loving than Scott "Bam Bam "Bigelow.

Shane calls those years "before the pills."

ERIC:
Hot dogs

ERIC BISCHOFF WAS working full-time for the AWA and still came home every day with regularity. He was tapped by Verne Gagne and Mike Shields to represent them in their syndication deals with TV networks airing the product. Montanna and Garett, two and three years-old at the time, saw dad regularly as he tried to revive a dying AWA product with TV deals.

The existing deals in place for the company were poor, with many being split revenue deals on advertising. Their crown jewel was a national cable deal with ESPN that had the product airing weekdays at 4 p.m. EST, putting it in kids' homes right after school. It brought the federation onto this Jersey kid's schedule, whereas prior my only exposure to it was in magazines and the malformed Pro Wrestling USA show, which had an AWA-heavy line-up.

What that ESPN deal did for the AWA as far as exposure, it failed to do financially. Gagne and Shields were wise to hire someone to shore up TV deals, because they were doing a dreadful job of landing big money advertisers. The company just couldn't monetize their barter deals and the stream they'd hoped would come in the form of live attendance just wasn't bridging the gap.

Eric had between 80 and 90 syndication outlets set up and the company just couldn't get out of its moribund state. The regional nature of the AWA, which worked well for Loree and the kids, did not for the company at a time when the territory system was all but dead. The McMahon WWE product redefined pro wrestling as a national game and despite the national exposure via ESPN, the AWA was still running live shows in their home loop in the Upper Midwest, namely Minnesota, Nebraska, Ohio, and Southern Illinois.

Eric didn't travel far from home all that much. He'd hit the major syndication cities, get them interested in the product, then make occasional follow-up visits and phone calls. Eric began showing up on-camera as well for the AWA television shows. He was still home all the time and wrestling, or AWA wrestling, was having no impact on his family life.

That should have been a tip-off as to where things were headed—an on-camera employee of a pro wrestling company in the sizzling late 80s that made it home every night. That double-edged sword, his being able to return to family every night but the company's inability to generate national money, would begin to cut. Eric began going weeks without a paycheck. He felt a loyalty to Verne that kept him working without the income.

"It just wasn't in my DNA to say, 'Sorry Verne—can't pay me, I'm gone," Eric says. "We'd become friends away from the business. We hunted together. I loved Verne." Those weeks without pay became months without pay. It was absolutely killing the Bischoff family financially. Eric had cars repossessed out of the driveway, and it hurt him to serve Montanna and Garett cut-up hot dogs yet again.

He was hanging on for Verne. Maybe they could turn it around. It was a blind faith in a man Eric respected greatly. But it was also ignoring a reality that was screaming loudly into his psyche, and he was doing it at the peril of his family. How long could they subsist heeding this loyalty?

Loree, for her part, stayed supportive. No doubt wearing a set of blinders as well, she knew there was a larger plan for Eric. Verne Gagne and the AWA were not the end-game, rather another step in the journey.

It was all sales, after all. Knock on that door, get that meeting, close it or not—and move on. Always move on. The next "close" could be down the street.

Down the street proved to be Atlanta, GA.

By 1992, the Gagne AWA was no longer and Eric was brought out east to serve as a 3rd and 4th string announcer for the national wrestling powerhouse, World Championship Wresting.

Well, powerhouse in the sense that the product was a firm, weekend stronghold on WTBS, Ted Turner's national superstation. After nearly a decade of the sport's national expansion and consolidation, WCW remained the only real coast-to-coast competitor to the monolithic WWE. WCW may have been deluding themselves into thinking they were holding competitive with the WWE.

As Eric knew firsthand, much as a superstation as TBS might have been, WCW was not covering as much of the country as WWE. Even in 1992, Eric wasn't finding many people in Minneapolis watching WTBS, or even knowing what it was, let alone the WCW product. When he landed on-camera for WCW television, a much larger stage than the AWA, he was still largely unknown back home. Certainly less so than when he was on TV for the local product. Eric had not even see a WCW show until he was called to audition.

After years of getting their asses kicked in the pocket book with Verne, the WCW job proved a Godsend, and a game changer. The family stresses over finances lifted, but herein began the next bumpy stretch of road—time away from home. Eric was now working for a company based in Atlanta, so he'd be on planes a lot. He'd fly into Atlanta on Sunday night to begin the workweek on Monday. He'd shoot his spots on Monday, Tuesday, and Wednesday morning, and be on a plane later on Wednesday back to Minneapolis. He'd have three or four days with the family, then do his three or four out in Atlanta.

For the first time, the Bischoff family was adjusting to a

schedule that saw Eric splitting his weeks between home and Atlanta. Admittedly, it was hard being away so much. But after the car repossessions and canned beans with hot dogs that come with working for the AWA, this was a challenge that yielded far more dividends than it lost.

The kids were the toughest part for Eric to reconcile, but he made it count when he was home. Montanna was getting into ballet and dance, so he made it a point to get to her events. Garett and Eric shared outdoor interests, and Eric made sure they had time for those.

He was making it work. Loree beside him, there was light at the end of the tunnel and, however improbable, that light was professional wresting—the oddball product that just may indeed have been the purest form of marketing in the world.

About six months after getting comfortable with WCW, real transition would come as the leadership saw Bischoff's contributions to the company could be greater than they were at the time. More demands were placed on him, his schedule expanded with those responsibilities, and the 8 and 9 year-old Montanna and Garett would have to sacrifice some more time away from daddy, in the exchange for more economic stability—which children know nothing of, nor care.

Six months after proving his worth at WCW, Eric Bischoff's salary had swelled from $0 in AWA, to $70,000 annually with the Atlanta-based company. After their previous few years, it felt like $370,000.

With this came an amped up schedule, seeing Eric head to Atlanta on Sunday, work Monday through Friday, and fly home to Minnesota on Friday, exhausted. Monday was TV at Center Stage—the production facility used for taping the show. Tuesday was another town, another syndicated TV shoot. Wednesday, Thursday, and usually Friday morning were studio days. He was more ensconced in the production of the shows, and increasingly proving his worth to the organization.

He was now away from home more, and after getting in late Friday night, he'd crash and sleep all day Saturday. Loree, Garett, and Montanna got him Sunday. For a bit. Then he was on a plane again, Atlanta bound. After just a few months of this, it began to take its toll. He'd get home and be shocked when seeing his own children.

"The kids looked like they aged three years," Eric says. "When they're really young they develop so quickly." He knew early on that the schedule, as it was, would not work long-term. The money was the lifting of a massive burden, but the wife and kids were simply too important.

"I wasn't going to wake up one day and realize my kids were driving themselves to school."

KEVIN:
Working is providing

BY SHEER COINCIDENCE Kevin Sullivan was working on a card just 12 miles from where his first child was ready to be born. Little Shannon Sullivan's first cries were ready to bounce down the halls of Cambridge Hospital in Massachusetts, and as fate would have it, he was wresting in nearby Concord. Sullivan was working for the venerable Vince J. McMahon's WWWF in 1976 so he was always in the Northeast anyway. But 12 miles away on the day of the birth—that was just great luck for the 26 year-old, Boston-Irish tough kid.

Kevin made it to the hospital with little effort and was there for Shannon's birth, as he would be for all of his children, regardless of where he worked. Being nearby to the hospital in 1976 was a coincidence, but future births were planned for.

In typical fashion for a blessed occasion of any kind in the life of a 70s pro wrestler, Sullivan had the day to spend with family and the new baby, but was out of the hospital parking lot and back on the road the next day. He didn't expect anything else, didn't actually need it.

"Back then parents were just about providing for the child," Sullivan says, "and they did that by working."

Sullivan spent all of 1976 working on the bottom half of cards for Vince Sr. and eventually moved on. By the time his second child, Ben, was born, the family found themselves in Tennessee, having moved out of Massachusetts when Kevin landed the gig working that territory. 1978 saw Benjamin's arrival come via the Volunteer State and it wouldn't be long before Kevin's career found a sweet spot—a territory wherein he would come into his own and make his home, workplace, and university under professor Eddie Graham.

Championship Wrestling from Florida brought Kevin down to Tampa where he'd make a name for himself as both a remarkably vicious heel, as well as a creative force in the business. Kevin would become known for a character whose identity would follow him for decades to come.

A couple of decades later when Kevin was in his mid-40s, fatherhood would again become a role he'd play, only by that point the business had changed significantly. In 1996 Kevin found himself working for the WCW, which was rapidly expanding and positioning itself as the worthy second-in-line to the massive WWE. Ratings wars were at fever pitch, with the two companies battling it out on the Monday night terrain.

Kevin's role as one of the men on the creative team for that company until its demise in 2001 kept him on the road more than he'd ever been. Territory travel days were one thing, sending you out on the weekly loop but bringing you home most nights. The national expansion of the wrestling product in the 80s saw to it that if you were a top star, you were going national with the company. If you were a booker, or later on a writer, then you were even more integral to the product. If you were both, like Sullivan, you were never coming home. Or at least it felt that way.

The new woman in Kevin's life, Linda, knew the deal before the 1996 birth of their lovely lady, Bianca. Linda was an athlete herself, a bodybuilder and powerlifter who knew first-hand of the demands of professional athletics. Still, it didn't make flying solo any easier. But she was down for the job.

"She was a rock," Kevin says of her at the time. She was holding it all together at home, while Kevin was trying to hold the flailing WCW together from the road. Home seemed a transient state.

"It's hard when you come home and crash on the couch, spend the second day lying around, and on the third day you're packing to go out the door."

The territory structures in New York, Tennessee, and Florida kept Kevin a drive away from home at all times. He was traveling most days and wrestling most nights back then, but Shannon and Ben saw more of him. The wrestling landscape of the 90s was the supersized version of that lifestyle. There was just nothing Kevin could do with the flight schedule and cut-throat atmosphere created by the weekly ratings contest, covered in-depth by wrestling publications and websites. Linda understood.

"It was very difficult to participate fully as a parent," Kevin admitted.

TITO:
Family first

OLE ANDERSON, ONE of wrestling's legendary bookers, has been responsible for many hours of wrestling's great angles and for making some stars like Tommy Rich. But from a personality standpoint, Ole was pretty universally known as a prick.

Tito Santana and his wife Leah, at 7 months pregnant, left Minnesota and bought a condo in Marietta, Georgia. The move was a lot to ask of her—rearranging her life while about to give birth—but Tito felt it was worth it to make the jump at that time. He'd spoken to Ole, the booker for Georgia Championship Wrestling at that time in the fall of 1982, and Ole promised Tito a big push and involvement in high-profile angles. Tito, Leah, and the coming baby could set up for a time in Georgia, based on what seemed would be a lengthy and successful stay working for Ole in Atlanta. They made the move into their new condominium.

A couple of months into his tenure in the Georgia territory, their first son, Matt, was born on December 27th. Tito was present at the hospital for the birth and while it was the happiest day of his life, there was also an unfortunate strain on the situation, courtesy of Ole. Tito made it clear to his new booker that he would be present for his baby's birth and be home for a week afterward with Leah and their new addition. The boss, though, disapproved.

But for Tito, the word *'boss'* extended only to the world of wrestling. He had a firm grip on things outside the ring.

"Ole was pretty controlling and didn't have a family life himself," Tito says. "He really didn't give a crap about his family. And when I told him I wanted to take a week off to be with my family, he wasn't very accepting." Some four-letter words flew about between Tito and Ole, but Tito was unrelenting in his decision. The territory would survive for a week without him. This was his *family*.

For Merced Solis, family was more important than anything else. He could become Tito Santana again in a few days. Matt was only going to be born once.

It was also easier for Tito's conscience to allow him to defy Ole's orders because the moon that was promised to Tito had remained in the sky thus far. Tito wasn't getting the push in Atlanta that was promised. When he would approach Ole about it, Ole's response was always the same—"Not yet, not yet." Tito tried to reason with the brusque booker.

"Ole, my wife just had a baby," he said to Ole. "We just bought a condominium. You made me promises and you're not keeping them." Ole showed no empathy. To him, this was the life of the wrestler. You want time off? Go be a teacher.

"He was just a cold hearted guy," said Tito. "He didn't care."

Back when Tito was initially weighing the move from Minnesota to Georgia, when Leah was already a few months pregnant, one thing that made the decision to uproot them a little easier was the pay guarantee. In the uncertain world of pro wrestling, a guarantee—a dependable minimum amount of money in your paycheck with room for upward movement—was the wrestler's dream. You could count on a steady salary. You weren't living solely based on how big arenas were. There was less risk when you were working on a guarantee.

But soon after arriving, that guarantee would prove to be just more of Ole's maneuverings.

"They worked the shit out of me," Tito began. "I came down there with a guarantee and he got rid of the guarantee, and I didn't have any control without a signed contract. Back then they used to treat the wrestlers like crap. Finally they got me to the point where they were booking me in Louisiana for Bill Watts and he was paying me pretty good."

Tito headed down to the Louisiana territory for promoter Bill Watts. Though cut from a similar hard-nosed mold as Ole, Watts had a fondness for legitimate athletes like himself, a former football player. Tito's football background fit with Watts's image of the pro wrestler. Tito was able to work the sprawling territory and make some good money there, as the area was doing great business at the turn of the decade.

Tito also had an ace up his sleeve. One of the wiser bits of wrestling business advice was once offered by legendary champion Harley Race to a young Rick Martel who, incidentally, would become Tito Santana's tag team partner in the late 1980s. Race told Rick, who'd just started in wrestling— "You have to take care of tomorrow's business today." It's advice that actually transcends pro wrestling and applies to far more than not. And the wiser men of the ring could be found thinking that way during the territory years.

Prior to his going to Louisiana, Tito was looking a few moves ahead and made an important phone call. Tales of wrestlers being bounced around the country carelessly and without strategy were plenty. Not every man who donned tights had the business mindset. Tito was a bright guy, though.

Vince J. McMahon's phone rang and the talented young man on the other end told him he was headed to Bill Watts's Mid-South Wrestling, but was already looking beyond that stint.

"Tito, it's time to come home," the senior McMahon said. It had been a couple of years since Tito worked the New York territory and after he wrapped up his commitments to Bill Watts in Louisiana, he would be headed back to the New York territory in the spring of 1983.

Things were changing up there. Vince's son, Vincent K. McMahon, was more and more becoming a central figure in the company, no longer just the TV announcer. That year, the company would be bought outright from Vince J. by his son and investors.

Tito returned to a WWE ring on his birthday—May 10, 1983. He never left again.

Tito's success in the new WWE would come very fast. Within a year of his return, the young McMahon saw to it that Tito was wearing a championship belt. In February of 1984, Tito won the WWE Intercontinental Championship—a title that he would become closely identified with as the WWE made its national expansion and took over the cable airwaves. Tito became a two-time Intercontinental Champion and had prominent feuds with "Magnificent" Don Muraco, Greg "The Hammer" Valentine, and Randy "Macho Man" Savage. Tito was the B-show main event in hundreds of towns per year, basically headlining any city that mega-star Hulk Hogan was not. He was having a great run.

Leah also loved the move back to the Northeast, as she was originally from New Jersey. They settled in the Garden State as Tito went back to the Connecticut-based company though, in actuality, by 1984 the company was no longer a territory operation. Cable TV and aggressive live show bookings spread Vince K. McMahon's federation across the entire country. Tito was a bona fide star in the company and was working all over the United States for the WWE, and overseas dates as well.

After Tito and Leah settled in New Jersey, their second son, Michael, came along. During the pregnancy, Leah's mother came up from Arizona to help out because Tito's road schedule was brutal. He had very little time at home and if Leah found herself in need, he'd most likely be away. This was critical time in Tito's career, as he was either defending or chasing the Intercontinental title all over the country. As Leah's due date neared, Tito's mother came up from Texas to help out as well.

As fate would have it, Tito was working in Baltimore the night of the birth—a driving shot for him, only a few hours from the family's New Jersey home. He could have very easily been working in California, Toronto, or Chicago. But fortune put him a mere three-hour ride from Leah.

Tito headed out of the Baltimore Civic Center and rode I-95 back home to New Jersey. He didn't even need to get out of the car. As soon as he pulled into the driveway, his mother came out of the house before he could get his bags out of the trunk.

"Merced," she began, "Leah just left with her mother to the hospital. She's going to have the baby." Tito pulled right back out of the driveway and headed to Morristown Hospital. When he got there he suited up in a hospital pullover and did a 'run-in' he'd never forget. The baby boy had just been delivered before he got there, and he walked in and saw Leah's mother holding the scissors to the umbilical cord, ready to cut.

"I let her do it," Tito said. He was selfless and family was truly the most important thing in the world to him. It was only natural he'd offer his mother-in-law a bond with her grandchild like that. He'd made it back from the card in Baltimore just in time, then made it to the hospital. Now the family was together to welcome little Michael into the world.

But the cold reality remained that Tito was working front and center in the growing WWE and his daily participation was integral. As crushing as it was to walk out of that hospital and back out onto the road with a newborn son in the hospital nursery, it had to be done.

"If we didn't wrestle, we didn't get paid," he says. "I was the main event in a lot of shows. I was a 'company guy.' The people wanted to see me wrestle and I kept my commitments."

A few years later, Tito's third son, Mark, was born. This time things were little different with regards to Tito's position in the company. He'd put in grueling man-hours and drawn good money as a B-show headliner. He'd proven himself and was one of Vince's most trusted soldiers. Tito was reliable, reasonable, and led a clean lifestyle. He was a huge asset to the WWE, in the ring and out.

So with that in mind, having served WWE so faithfully in Vince's most important growth years, Tito asked for the time off to be with Leah for the birth of Mark, which he was granted. Fittingly, Tito was at the hospital for the births of all three children during the busiest time in wrestling's history. He aptly served his duty as both company man, as well as family man.

JJ:
A cry

TWO YOUNG GIRLS, ages 8 and 10, were rendered without a mother the moment police walked into the apartment. The kids weren't home, but police discovered two adults, a man and woman, laid out with spikes still in their arms. Medics arrived and immediately started working on the two moribund adults. They get the male going again. The lady was gone. Two little girls' lives are now forever the unthinkable.

All the children that came into JJ Dillon's life did so in manners as atypical and varied as the career and marriages he'd chosen. There were births—both easy, and difficult. There were stepchildren, assumed upon marriage to someone with kids. There were step-nieces, taken in and raised like his own. There was even an unexpected pregnancy at age 52.

Like any good wrestling angle, JJ was keeping friends and

family tuning in and guessing what on earth was next. Let no one lose sight of the fact that three of those children came to be after the successful and improbable comeback from a vasectomy. That is some Attitude Era shit.

JJ is an easy going guy, and he was along for this ride from the moment he chose pro wrestling, or perhaps, it chose him.

"If you were going to write all this as a novel, people would go, 'That's farfetched,'" he says. "I don't know. I guess from being around the wrestling business for so long I wasn't phased by anything."

After JJ's first marriage, the four-year stint with Lynda, and the natural childbirth of his first daughter, Pam, there came his three stepsons from his second wife Jeanette's prior marriage. Career-wise, things start kicking into gear when he married Jeanette. He was working in Detroit for The Sheik Ed Farhat at the time and is also working for the Australian wrestling promotion in 1979.

Extensive wrestling travel wasn't an issue from a parenting standpoint because little Pam was with ex-wife Lynda and her new husband, and JJ's current wife Jeanette's boys were away at a private school, funded for children without present fathers. They were away, as was JJ, for extended stretches of time. By the time Australia came calling, the boys were out of school and Jeanette was able to pack up and move in with JJ Down Under for a time.

JJ never formed a closeness with Jeanette's three boys as they were away at school most of the time, and when they got out they went right to work on their own paths, forming their own lives. The youngest one did live with JJ and Jeanette for a time, so there was some cursory connection there.

"Of the three boys, with the oldest one, there's not much of a relationship," JJ began. "The middle one, some. There was a little bit of a relationship with the youngest. He lived with us for a while then he went into the Navy."

After the boys moved on, the Morrison home would not so quickly assume the cavernous, empty nest aura. Jeanette and JJ would soon make the decision to raise two young girls, brought to them by tragic circumstances.

Jeanette's sister was on her second marriage. She was living in Pennsylvania with her husband, a disabled veteran, and they both developed a habit. Police found her and her husband unresponsive, with syringes jammed in their veins. Though he was resuscitated by paramedics, Jeanette's sister was pronounced dead at the scene. Jeanette's little nieces were now without a mother and stepfather, and consequently a massive burden fell onto her former brother-in-law, the girls' biological father. It was a challenge he couldn't answer at the time.

JJ and Jeanette decided at once to take the girls. Their father was simply not going to be able to provide for them on his own. It wasn't for lack of love. He was simply not in a position to do it, and JJ, finding mounting success in wrestling, could. They proposed it to Jeanette's former brother-in-law and he agreed to let the girls move to Kansas City, where JJ and Jeanette were living at the time. As JJ tells it, they immediately created a nuclear home for the girls.

"Wherever we went, they went," JJ says. "We raised them

like they were our own children." Yet another twist and turn, met by JJ with the casual acceptance of a life atypical.

Though JJ's first child, Pam, was living with her mom, Lynda, and her stepfather, when JJ was working the Dallas and Kansas City territories, she would come and stay with him. He ensured he was getting time with her as well.

His 17-year marriage to Jeanette would eventually come to an end after his having helped on a limited basis with three stepsons, and in a full-time capacity with raising Jeanette's two nieces.

Enter Lindsey.

In his 50th year, his work partner in WCW's travel department would soon become his partner in life. They wed and soon her desire to have children prompted JJ to head back to Dallas and visit the doctor who eleven years prior performed his vasectomy. Years prior, just before the initial procedure, the doctor gave his standard, pre-op speech.

"This is permanent," he told JJ. "When you make this decision it should be with the idea in mind that you don't want to have children."

JJ remembers the doctor smiling when he walked into that same doctor's office eleven years later.

"I had that first conversation with all my patients," the doctor began, "and you're not the first to come back asking 'what are the chances?'"

That reversal, along with Lindsey's fertility treatments,

proved successful and soon enough she was pregnant with twins. A Monday morning found Lindsey and JJ in the hospital and beautiful, little Amanda's special day was created. Her counterpart and nine month roommate, though, was having trouble. Geoffrey, the second twin, was in crisis and the team of doctors finally brought him out after remaining far too long in the womb and suffering a loss of oxygen.

Little Geoffrey was unresponsive and the medical team rushed him to the other side of the room as Lindsey and JJ breathlessly waited. The bed of noise in the room was a symphony of tools, meters, low voices, and scurry.

Then, a cry.

Never before or since has JJ been so happy to hear a child wail. They did it. Geoffrey was alive. The near-miracle came with a price—Geoffrey would have to learn to live with Cerebral Palsy. The difficulties at birth had compromised the functionality of the left side of his body. He would be wheelchair bound. But Lord, he was alive. Looking back at the event, now twenty-five years past, JJ is still gripped at the throat. He tears up and composes himself when recounting the hours in the hospital, the grim uncertainty, and handicapping of his only son.

"We almost lost him. He was in neonatal ICU for three weeks."

The wrestling machine never stops cranking and perhaps there is some benefit to getting lost in your work after a harrowing event. JJ was not on the road but went to the WCW office every day. He never stopped working during or after the birth of the twins. Not really sure that was even an option in the wrestling business.

After a lifetime working the professional wrestling circuit without landing in the sports' largest federation, operated in JJ's former backyard in the Northeast, the WWE finally became a reality for him.

A little more than a year after the birth of his twins, JJ found himself working for Vince McMahon's WWE, his former boss's archenemy. JJ's work for WWE was entirely behind the scenes, working for the office. The sprawling federation had become a massive corporate entity by the 1990s. He was sent to Japan by Vince to help handle an important deal that was in the works. For years Vince had a working agreement with Giant Baba's All Japan Pro Wrestling, but now Vince wanted to expand and open up Japan as a market for WWE and WWE alone. He wanted to run Japan as an outside promotion.

JJ boarded the plane to help with the particulars, utilizing connections he'd made in Japan over the years. Lindsey, home with the twins, called with some peculiar news.

She was pregnant again.

JJ told her there had to be a mistake. They'd tried for two years with the twins, complete with both of them getting some medical assistance in the process. Lindsey had needed fertility drugs for the pregnancy. The two hadn't necessarily been concerned about birth control in the past year. What the hell would the odds be, given all the complications prior? He told her to get another test.

She did. She was pregnant.

He'd be able to spend more time at home now that he was working exclusively in the WWE office. TV and pay-per-view events required that he be on-hand, but generally he wouldn't be away for more than two or three-day stretches.

Now, at 52 years-old, JJ would become a father once again.

VINCE:
The nanny

VINCE RUSSO WAS standing in the back of a darkened movie theater whispering into his cell phone, trying to be heard above the explosions on the screen. He was getting stares aplenty from the surrounding Saturday afternoon movie-goers.

A nice thing about being the head writer of the biggest wrestling TV shows in the country, as opposed to being a wrestler on them, is your travel is easier. TV still shot on only prescribed days whereas house shows, non-televised wrestling cards, went on all damn week long. Wrestlers worked on TV, then they worked on the house shows. A week later, they worked on TV again, followed by more house shows. Following week? Right.

Vince Russo was writing what we saw on *WWE RAW* and *Smackdown* during their prime years. There were also less significant TV shows the company aired, also shot on *RAW* and *Smackdown* days. It was hours and hours of TV for which Russo was responsible. But as far as physical travel, he found himself at arenas for Monday and Tuesday TV, with the occasional Sunday pay-per-view, which happened a dozen times a year. In essence, his travel schedule was the same as when he'd put himself on the road for TV tapings as editor of the WWE Magazine.

While physically in Connecticut, his mind and heart had been stolen from his body by Vince McMahon. The WWE product was on fire, having been given a healthy second life after a desiccated stretch in the early 90s riddled with legal wrangling and scandal. McMahon found himself in courtrooms, on talk show sets, in addition to the arenas. And there was more interest in the prior than the latter. The McMahon family business was anemic at that time.

The edgy WWE product of the second half of the 1990s gave an endorphin blast to the company's collapsing veins. Superstars were again being born in its rings and on its TV. Money was flowing in. TV contracts were hotly pursued by networks. Life, anew. Excess, actually.

Vince Russo was writing it, along with his namesake McMahon. He'd given Russo the ball in desperate times, and now he was wearing the company jersey, the starting quarterback on the team that looked like it was headed to the Super Bowl. McMahon knows a good thing when he sees one. He built a company on looking across the room and getting the pretty girl to dance with him, right out of the arms of her date, at times. Hogan stands up Verne. JYD stands up Watts.

You could go on all day. McMahon might not make them, but he knows them when he sees them. And when he gets them, he works them hard. The stream of WWE Attitude era revenue was flowing in the blood let from the veins of Austin, Rock, Foley, Russo, and McMahon. Let it never be said that McMahon didn't sacrifice as much as his stars, put in as much time as his writers and bookers.

That commitment from McMahon himself required inhumane time commitment from head writer Vince Russo. The fact that he wasn't on the road for TV did nothing to curb the amount of time he was being pulled from home and family. He felt like he lived in the WWE offices, and now his phone rang constantly in the few hours he wasn't actually there.

Like during this matinee movie. It would be unthinkable to not answer the phone when McMahon's number was on the display. Russo couldn't leave his two young boys alone in the theatre, so he scrambled to the back of the auditorium and answered. Vince wanted to talk. And talk. You or I might be able to get off a phone call in a minute or so with a quick, "Hey listen, let me get back to you later. I'm in a movie theatre with my kids."

Not with McMahon.

Oh, Russo said where where he was. He told McMahon in an effort to explain away the sounds of battle on-screen. McMahon talked right through the explanation, as if he didn't even hear it. Probably didn't.

It was par for the course on a weekend. If Russo had the

temerity to plan an activity with Amy, Will, V.J., and Annie for a Saturday at 11 a.m., invariably that phone would ring at 9. It would be McMahon.

"I need you in the office at ten," he would say. And that was it.

"Vince [McMahon] did not give a shit about your family," Russo said. "When he wanted you, you had to jump. That's what was expected of you." Should it matter to the head of a multi-million dollar entity that his head writer spent three days traveling with the show, then the next three days in the office working until well into the darkness?

One day. Saturday. Russo saw opportunity in his one morning at home to get a couple of hours with Amy and the kids. He wasn't an idiot—he knew there would be calls from Stamford on a Saturday. He'd answer them, talk about the upcoming TV angles with Vince. But he'd be out with his family.

One friggin' day. Not even. Half-a-day.

"Amy, I gotta go in." She'd look down and nod, just like he looked away when he said it. Her face was enough. Little Annie's might paralyze him.

"The job came before the family," Russo says. He swallows as much blame himself as he serves to McMahon. "At that time, I was so caught up in the bubble of the business, I was just rolling with it. I just wanted to be the absolute best. It's not that I was a mark for the wrestling business. That's not what drove me. I just wanted to be the absolute best at what I did."

There was no desire for TV sales superstardom at P.C.

Richard & Sons. He just worked to overachieve. And that meant if he was shilling Panasonics, he'd try and shill the most. If *WWE RAW* nailed a 4.9 rating last week, he wanted a 5.0 this week. It's a personality type that makes for good coaches and generals, though absentee fathers.

The strain showed in Amy. Her phrase that haunts him today was uttered more than once. He remembers each instance.

"I'm a single parent," she said.

While it carried the sting of a smack across the face, he couldn't fight it. He knew he was an extension of a company, 24/7. Though not who Amy married, it was who he was now. He knew it.

"There was just no backing off that you had to commit your life to that company," Russo says. "And that's literally what happened."

The duality of feeding his need to achieve but also his family and their happiness forced him into McMahon's office with a plan one day. Annie was getting older and Amy was now firmly raising three growing children alone. Russo had a good thing going at WWE and providing is a big part of parenting.

Though, not the only part.

He told McMahon he wanted to move Amy closer to her family. They could help her out when she needed it because he could be of zero help as long as McMahon was awake. Russo wasn't looking for sympathy from his high-profile boss—that would be both ridiculous and unreasonable. How about an understanding moment or gesture? That might be an elixir Russo would welcome. An, *"I get it, pal. Been there myself."* Could happen.

"I don't understand," McMahon said to Russo. "You make a lot of money now. Why don't you get a nanny to watch your kids."

As far as emotionally explosive turning points go, that was Russo's Mount Vesuvius. He knew, sitting right in McMahon's office, that he could not work one more day for the man across the desk.

"Right there I realized this man doesn't give a shit about me or about my family."

McMahon made a logical attempt to solve the problem put before him. He likely didn't mean insult. He's been described as a calculated dictator, cold and unwavering in the face of a task.

Childcare issues? Nanny. Solved.

And for some that may have been the answer. Certainly,

anyone cut from the same cloth as McMahon would see it that way. And why not? Childcare assistance is a massive and legitimate industry servicing millions of parents that have no choice. There is no shame in it.

But Russo was troubled by the distance from his kids as it was. It was a touchy subject and in all likelihood the gesture of Vince moving the Russos a little closer to Amy's family would have been sufficient, whether or not they actually took him up on it. But he didn't offer it, and his head writer bristled at his alternate suggestion, seeing it as cold and dismissive.

Russo has called himself a proud Italian, invoking the image of a public smack across the cheek. Pride would not allow him to stomach the insult. He may have decided on his own to sell his family short for a career pursuit, but there was no way some other guy was going to do it. Didn't matter what his last name was.

These wrestling fathers found themselves answering the call of the business nearly hours after the birth of their children. Though it would be years until the concept of the paternity leave took hold, most jobs offered some flexibility A new father could expect a couple of days off from the assembly line or the office.

After the births, the wrestlers were booked somewhere the following night, so it was out the door. Considering wrestling took the men all over the road, it is surprising to see how many of them actually got to the delivery of the children. Luck, it seems, found these road warriors.

Tito Santana happened to get home after a Baltimore shot just as Leah was taken to the hospital to deliver their first child, so there's some luck of the draw there. If he had been working in Boston with a shot in Maine the next day, he wouldn't have been able to get back to New Jersey.

Kevin Sullivan wrestled 12 miles away from the hospital where his first child was born. He made it. So did Lanny Poffo. JJ Dillon and Eric Bischoff were not yet doing the wrestling grind, so they were there for the births of their first children. As wrestlers stayed in the business longer and acquired more clout, they could arrange to be on hand for any subsequent births.

Workers with the most haggard schedules so greatly valued their time at home that they've spoken of overcompensating and making that time valuable. From Gary Hart, to Bam Bam Bigelow, to Eric Bischoff, to Vince Russo, we heard about these workers "making it count" when they were home. Lanny Poffo bought Magen nice gifts from the road. All identified the time away as time stolen from the kids.

Tony Atlas's story is particularly heartbreaking because of the physical distance between he and Nikki. Tony didn't have the opportunity that the others did. Wrestling and fatherhood could not co-exist for him and Joyce, it seems.

The cornerstone of the stories we are exploring seems to be the wife. Not enough can be said of the wrestling wife in the success or failure of the wrestling father. If she knew the deal, knew what was expected of her husband in his role of wrestling star, and was of Goddess-like construction herself, she could shoulder the burden at home. It would be lonely. It would be maddening to handle the children alone. But if they were on the crazy train *with* their husbands, then they had a shot.

Then it was in the hands of the worker to screw up. Keeping a wife on the team is a lot easier when you don't add addiction and extramarital endeavors into the mix, it would seem. So the Bischoffs, Russos, Poffos, and Santanas of the world seemed to have the advantage.

Children knowing that they are a working parent's first priority and that, if need be, the parent would throw it all away for them, is usually enough to secure them. They missed daddy, but when they next had occasion to see his face if it lit up like the world depended on them, burnt foliage would fall away.

There were workers not profiled here, who have stated publicly that the minute they got home, they couldn't wait to get back out the door. They yearned to be away from their wife and kids, start drinking and partying again, and they made it no secret to the folks at home. It's fucked up, and no doubt those kids grew up fucked up as well. I don't know all their names, but find a few and let me know how those kids are doing.

It just so happens that our crew of subjects for this project let everyone at home know the opposite. The kids would hear how these hours before the next flight out were paramount.

Home, not the Garden, was dad's main event.

3.

SMARTENING UP

"I HOPE MY KID is smart."

We've all said it. Most of us try and do something about it, help that process along. But when it comes to the machinations of the wrestling business, smartening up your kid takes on a whole new meaning. And questions.

Is it a betrayal to the wrestling business to expose the illusion to your own flesh and blood? And why bother doing it anyway? What's the harm in their believing they're watching their father in a legitimate athletic contest? There would eventually come a day when the "fake" word would be uttered at school anyway. They're gonna have to deal with it.

Keeping context is once again important here. The term

sports entertainment has become enmeshed in the lexicon of the wrestling fan, so any debate about the validity of a pro wrestling contest today would be ridiculous. We know what it is. Fans still celebrate the pageantry and daredevil-like performances, but no one alive and out of grade school feels wrestling is anything less than a work.

The years we are discussing in this study are that of a different time, and not just because the calendar says so. Pro wrestling was presented as spontaneous contest. There was great effort made to have you at home and you in the front row become passionately invested in the characters and the contests. For all intents and purposes, it worked because *they* were real. Maybe the finishes weren't, maybe selling wasn't. But damn your soul if you were going to stand before Steve "Dr. Death" Williams and put forth the idea that he wasn't the real deal.

So in that time, the blood spouting from a wrestler's head was real and that chair over his head sure looked and sounded real as well. There were a host of people standing and cheering that assault, poised to throw up a middle finger and tell the bloodied wrestler to go fuck himself as he left the ring. He was a heel, after all. A real bad dude.

And he was someone's dad.

So if the kids are coming to the matches or watching on TV, wouldn't there have to be *some* discussion about this beforehand? And even if they weren't going to see what daddy did at work, there would be plenty of kids at school to fill them in.

There was also the old-school code of *kayfabe*, protecting the business and its secrets at all costs, that applied even to family in some wrestling homes. Kayfabe was upheld and enforced in the sphere around the wrestling business, but the diligence with which that was carried into the home varied from worker to worker.

JASON:
A fine lesson

GARY HART WALKED into the World Class Championship Wrestling locker room in 1984 with 7 year-old Jason in tow. It was another night in the Dallas territory but Gary had some extra pep in his step.

"Hey fellas," Gary called out to the room, getting the attention of the heel workers, in various states of undress and relaxation. "Just want to let you know that yesterday some kid was cracking on the business and my man Jason bloodied his fucking nose!"

There stood Jason—initially almost invisible in a room beside Kamala, the Freebirds, Skandor Akbar and the green-faced Missing Link. Instantly that little kid swelled five times his size. The locker room broke out in hearty applause. The boys came to center from all corners of the room and congratulated him, tussling his hair and hi-fiving him. It was like the mobster that got his first pinch.

In a twisted rite of passage, if you were in the wrestling business in the kayfabe years, you were expected to fight for real to protect it. Workers were tested in bars, clubs, and pool halls all over the country. The only battles a wrestler had to endure with outcomes not pre-arranged were those against the marks.

Fighting outsiders who publicly challenged the legitimacy of the business was so important to some owners and promoters that you'd be fired if you lost a bar fight to an unruly mark. Promoter Bill Watts carried a notorious reputation for having the *win-or-walk* policy for his Louisiana Mid-South territory. But regardless of a promoters policy, the wrestler of yesteryear carried with him or her a pride that demanded they preserve their honor by any means. A couple of beer-bellied truckers loudly proclaiming that the fake wrestlers over there couldn't fight for shit would not be open to much discussion anyway. You were obligated to change that opinion in the eyes of all in that pub.

But here's a 7-year-old kid. Concepts like *honor* and *protecting the business* were surely out of his universe. But how noteworthy that another kid in school simply saying, "wrestling is fake" spurred this instinctive reaction. Gary hadn't ever told Jason to fight. Jason just knew the seriousness with which he should take the bad-mouthing of the sport.

Those occasions were rare for the Williams boys. Most of the kids Jason interacted with in his schools were his friends and either didn't know who Jason's dad was, or didn't care very much. It just wasn't noteworthy conversation for them.

The times when Jason had to fight off little rednecks weren't reserved only for instances when they were saying the sport was bullshit. The opposite end of that spectrum was also problematic for the son of a heel manager–when the kids believed *too* much. When Gary or one of his proteges did something heinous to one of the insanely popular Von Erich boys, his son would be a very accessible target for a pissed off 8-year-old fan of the babyfaces.

Those fights were expected and Jason just dealt with them as they arose. He'd been subconsciously groomed like a pit bull—always be ready to bite. For years he'd been out with dad and seen first-hand the liberties fans sometimes took with heels. Overzealous babyface fans certainly had the propensity to act like heels themselves when coming face to face with Gary.

Children generally don't see their parents being hated by the general public. The average kid would bristle at some kid on the block calling their dad "fat" or "stupid." Jason regularly saw packs of fans verbally attack his father on the streets in everyday situations, and *thousands* do it in arenas. And while that heat in the arenas was part of the deal and came with dad's act, the impromptu confrontations while out at the dry cleaner, supermarket, or during a family outing were nerve-wracking. That anxiety followed Jason out the door with Gary whenever they went out for any reason

Anxiety related to a parent's safety at the hands of society at large is a very unique and rare condition for a young child. Such difficulty is seen in children with parents in select fields of work—law enforcement, military, and politics being the most common. A kid can lose that sense of safety that should surround their home, putting them on an emotional roller coaster. They fear what could happen to mom or dad when they're off at work, and they fear what could happen to themselves when they're just with mom or dad.

In 1983 when Jason was 6 years-old, he was riding in dad's car with Gary and his protege The Great Kabuki. They were headed to work a wrestling card for the Carolina's Mid-Atlantic territory. As they were pulling down an off-ramp in Charlotte, North Carolina, Gary saw a congregation of fans in the arena parking lot which lay just off the exit. Gary turned to Kabuki, the Japanese heel who spoke little English, and gave him a signal.

"Song-Song," Gary said. Kabuki threw on a chain metal mask he used to cover his face when not done up in his trademark face paint. Fans were not to see Kabuki's face. He was a character shrouded in mystery and humanizing him would kill the gimmick.

Incidentally, the command *Song-Song* was a tribute to Pak Song, a Korean heel also managed by Gary, who died a couple of years prior. It became a generic call of instruction from Gary to his Asian protégés. It simply meant whatever was obvious and needed at the time. Gary tapping Kabuki and pointing to the assembly of fans near the entrance and saying, *"Song-Song"* obviously meant it was time to cover his face from the marks. In the ring, if they were going to time a spot where Kabuki would spit his blinding, green mist into the face of his opponent, when the referee turned his back Gary could call out *"Song-Song."*

On this afternoon though, it simply meant "cover up." Kabuki did so and Gary was soon parked near the entrance. There was still a walk through the fans to the door and the safety of a locker room filled with dangerous, hairy rule-breakers. Sanctuary.

The short walk to the door had barricades on either side to keep fans back, allowing talent to enter the building unobstructed. Gary, Kabuki, and little Jason exited the car and walked toward the door. Fans, though initially behind the barricades, began insulting the heels and the tiny heel-by-association, eventually leaning over the barricade to take a swing. Things were being tossed at the bad guys, from a distance of mere feet. Gary and Kabuki, professional villains who'd seen it all, kept their stride, walking cocky and unaffected. When it became apparent the distance was keeping the heels safe, the barricades were breached and some rowdies spilled into the walkway, ready to rumble.

Today's wrestling fan may not be able to comprehend the degree to which a particularly diabolical heel of yesteryear would incite unreasonably passionate fans. It wasn't a tongue-in-cheek dislike of someone playing a part, and doing it well. There was a subsection of fan that would and *did* try and do great harm to bad guys that they determined needed to be taken care of. And since these guys kept escaping the clutches of the referee with no real authority and a wrestling governing body that didn't exist, then they had to take the law of the ring into the own hands.

Jason could not believe that these guys were in no way considering that a 6 year-old boy was there. This group of hoodlums was charging the heel team and swinging real punches. It would have been easy for the youngster to have received a wayward strike in the fracas. Kabuki pulled out his nunchucks and he was wicked fast with them. A few swings and maybe a connection or two with a tipsy attacker's head cleared the path for the few seconds it took for all three to get inside.

Gary and Kabuki just went inside and went about their business. Joe Average would need a seat and an hour to stabilize his heart rate if attacked by a small, angry mob. Jason watched his dad and Kabuki get to work getting ready for the show, not rattled. Who knows what was going on inside the two men, but Jason saw the steely facade. That was equally as perplexing to him as the fan that would risk it all by hopping a guard rail in the presence of security and charge a couple of dangerous heels and a small child.

Neither was Gary's personal time with family immune to intrusions of an unpleasant nature. In 1987 when exiting a showing of the film *The Untouchables* with his wife and two boys, Gary was noticed by a couple of young men. When the family hit the sidewalk in front of the theatre, the guys made it known that they recognized the heel manager. They were creative and downright poetic.

"Fuck you, Gary Hart!" they shouted. Jason and Chad looked up at their dad. Twinkle sighed. Not her first rodeo. Gary turned to his family.

"Why don't you guys hang in the lobby for a second," he said. "I'm gonna go and pull up the car." Gary walked past the guys who were now getting into their Chevy IROC-Z near the entrance. It was a hairy situation for everyone. Jason was hoping those guys would just hurry up and drive off before they had to go outside to dad's car.

It didn't work out that way. Gary pulled up in his large Buick, positioning it right beside the hoodlums' car. They were carrying-on amongst themselves and didn't notice Gary.

He put the car in park. With a business-as-usual facade, he violently threw his large door open several times, repeatedly smashing it into the marks' sports car. The goof balls dove across their seats, shocked by the attack. *BANG-BANG-*

BANG.

Gary slid out and leaned into the scared teens' window. His eyes were ready to jump from his face. The tall manager kept sliding into their car menacingly as they cowered. His long slither never seemed to end. At last he stopped.

"I will cut your fucking dicks off," he said, flashing a prop. He checked their eyes and made sure he would be remembered. It was effective.

He turned from their car and calmly walked to his family who were watching intently from the theatre lobby.

"Okay, guys. Let's go." He led them to his car as the IROC pulled off. He put his family in and walked around to the driver's side. He assessed his door. It held up well and any war wounds were well worth the battle. He got in the car.

"Gary," Twinkle began. "Did you have to do that with the car?"

"That was a fine lesson for those two boys," Gary said. "Don't mess with old people."

He pulled off into the night, more than a little affected by watching DeNiro as Al Capone.

LANNY:
Daddy up

LITTLE MAGEN POFFO, holding her favorite doll brought home by daddy after a road trip, stood before the TV set, her bottom lip quivering.

"Daddy! Up! Daddy up!" She was beginning to get upset, hollering at the TV. On it was displayed a violent ballet that saw her daddy prone on the powder blue, WWE mat, beaten down by a heel. Magen was powerless and she didn't like it.

Daddy was home, though, in the living room. He was okay now. But that big TV was showing bad, bad things that happened to her daddy in some city, in a big ring. He was down and he was hurt.

Lanny saw her broken heart and a decision was made on the spot. He would decide to operate against the practices and beliefs of Angelo, and instead come from a place of instinct.

Lanny, for the umpteenth time, would forego the responsibility of being a *wrestling* father, and instead follow his heart and don the tights of just *father*.

"Sweetie," he said, sliding down on the carpet beside her. "Daddy is only playing on TV."

"Play?" she managed.

"Yes. I'm playing. Like *you* play." She was now listening intently. He had landed on a real-life teachable moment. Lanny, never one to shy away from theatrics, seized the moment. "Watch this, Magen."

Lanny moved some toys aside, clearing an area of living room rug. He took Magen by the hand and led her to the center of the clearing.

"Okay, Magen, take this hand, and throw a punch at daddy. Like this." He balled her fist.

Magen threw a timid little swat at her hero, who flew backward, taking every wrestling dad's expository bump that draws the big curtain back for their kids.

And like that, after a chuckle and a smile, Magen was smartened up.

Lanny sold the vicious, tiny strike, then rolled up and smiled at her.

"Fun?" he asked. She smiled and nodded. It was the perfect way to disarm the images on TV and set her little mind at ease. Some long-winded explanation about work, and the business, and some half-cocked attempt to protect the business would have been meaningless to Lanny's little girl with the tears in her eyes. That ten-second charade got a laugh, cessation of tears, and an understanding that never had to be explained again.

Lanny told her not to worry about it anymore.

"Because when I was young, *I* worried about it," Lanny said.

When Lanny was little and on the road with Angelo, he would sit in the front row of wrestling matches. He'd watch closely and began to figure something out. There was something about how these guys were fighting. On occasion, young Lanny also thought he could *hear* something between these guys as well. Their mouths were moving while they clenched, in tight.

There was, of course, no confirmation from his father or any of the workers. Lanny was putting it all together by watching Angelo and his co-workers pound at each other nightly. When he really looked at that pounding and listened closely, he knew the lights and the audience were just parts of a greater show happening before him. He'd eventually ask Angelo for confirmation of this. But Angelo certainly wasn't serving it up unprompted.

"Angelo would have died before he'd admit what I admitted to Magen." Though as he and Randy got older, the subject was broached with confirmation from Angelo that the sport was more like cooperation than competition.

Was that true for every *wrestler?* Lanny wondered. One wrestler came to mind when Lanny considered that question. He remembered seeing the flowing, blonde locks of one vicious heel in particular, bouncing under the hot lights as he dropped forearms onto waiting flesh. There was nothing, *nothing,* about the forearms that suggested anything less than pain was being doled out. There was absolutely *nothing* in this man's eyes that was soft, kind, or less than bent on destruction. Maybe all those other guys on the card, Angelo included, had that working agreement that Angelo confirmed.

Certainly, there was nothing fake about Johnny Valentine.

Lanny was pretty astute as a young observer of the sport, but Valentine seemed like the real deal. Lanny even asked Angelo if Valentine was really part of the work.

"Yeah, him too," Angelo replied. "He's just better than us."

ERIC:
Executives' kids don't need smartening up

HULK HOGAN SAT on the phone in his office going over potential finishes with Roddy Piper. The two workers had wrestled each other before, quite high profile, in another federation. It took care to make what was old, new again. Hogan was a craftsman and the highest profile worker in the history of the business.

A 13 year-old Garett Bischoff sat in the office listening to Hogan and the Scotsman, soon to be his opponent. Garett just happened to be spending time with one of his dad's friends, hanging out while dad was busy.

Hearing the details of what was to go on in a ring and the decisions that draw out angles and make them ratings draws was common background noise. Eric had climbed Turner's ladder at WCW, going from TV announcer, to Executive Producer, to

Vice President, and finally President. Garett and Montanna were around the business of the business all the time—from Eric taking calls at home at eleven or twelve at night, to Garett spending time around the production of the WCW television shows.

The Bischoff kids never had to learn to be smartened up. Osmosis was the teacher, as has been the case with most of the wrestlers' kids in this study. The children of most of the pro wrestlers saw gaps in reality by watching their dads work in the ring and by being around the locker rooms. They saw illusion under the hot lights and in the camaraderie between individuals who were supposed to be mortal enemies.

Montanna and Brooke Hogan   **Nick Hogan and Garett**

The unique aspect of the Bischoff kids' education is that it was all gleaned from growing up around the very top of a multi-million dollar corporate wrestling organization. It wasn't the wrestlers' locker room chatter, though they certainly saw their fair share of that too, that educated them. Rather, hearing dad's large-scale decisions about television contracts, quarter-hour ratings points, and talent direction smartened up Garett and Montanna beyond anything a sweaty locker room could have accomplished.

"My son knew more about the business by the time he was 16 years-old than anyone in TNA combined," Eric began, "simply because of his proximity to the discussion he heard me having. My kids heard more discussion about the business of the wrestling business by the time they were 15 years-old than people in the business do in a decade."

Garett in particular was a very social kid, preferring to hang out with the talent behind the scenes when he was in the arenas with Eric. When he was 12, 13, and 14 he could be seen killing time with Hogan, Sting, Savage, or the Nasty Boys backstage at the tapings. The worldly young man wasn't starstruck and knew how to talk with people of all ages and social strata. He was comfortable with people older than he, and as a result the talent at WCW came to see Garett as a buddy, and not the boss' kid.

The neighborhood kids that hung out with Garett and Montanna generally knew the deal as well. Many of them talked cars or motorcycles with Mr. Bischoff when visiting the house. They weren't fazed by the wrestling thing, and none of them thought Garett's dad was the scumbag leader of some NWO faction of villains. The Bischoff kids' friends liked Eric and thought hanging around the heel executive on TV was pretty badass.

One of their young friends, a girl named Amy, was dealing with some heavy issues at home. The instability in her household caused her mother to reach out to Eric and Loree for help. The girl was becoming deeply affected by the tumult, finding herself without many friends and lacking confidence.

Eric and Loree took Amy in on many occasions, keeping her sheltered from what was going on in her home, while also allowing her to live in the warmth of Montanna's and Garertt's friendship. She lived with them for a couple of years, on and off.

Eric took her to TV tapings when his kids would come. She'd hang with the talent, take pictures with Hogan, and see how big time wrestling TV was produced.

Amy and Hulk

It would be pretty tough for Eric Bischoff, now the leader of the diabolical New World Order, to live the gimmick while giving a troubled young girl a stable home. Good thing it was the 90s.

JASON:
Ric lost to a bullshit hold

9 YEAR-OLD JASON stood in the middle of a bloody fracas. He was scared. There was a 400 lb. man with reservoir-deep gashes running vertically down his bald head, grunting and moaning in what may have been Sudanese Arabic. He'd just been chased up the aisle by a bearded, wild man in fur-lined boots, with Jason's dad in tow. The gang of wrestlers was already in the back, out of sight and earshot of fans. Yet, Gary Hart was still screaming at referee David Manning.

"It's because he's black, ain't it?!" Gary was shouting. "It's because he's *black!* If he was white you'd have no problem!" Gary and Manning were carrying on in the locker room corridor of the arena. Abdullah the Butcher and Bruiser Brody had already ducked into the dressing rooms. But Gary and Manning kept at it in the corridor.

Jason was scared *not* by the brawl that he'd followed up the aisle through the bloodthirsty and terrified fans. Abdullah scared everyone, but not Jason. Dad did look pretty mad now, but he wasn't even afraid of Gary.

He was afraid *for* him.

Referee David Manning wasn't backing down. He was in Gary's face yelling back.

"He hit me first, Hart!"

Manning looked mad. Now the cops would certainly come and probably arrest dad. He'd yelled at a *referee*. They were in big trouble now.

At 9 years-old, Jason already knew the deal about what went on inside the ring. And, occasionally, up the aisle and into the back. Jason considered himself "with it." All these guys were dad's friends and he never really worried about the beatings or wins and losses. The workers were all cool with each other and with either winning or losing.

But those *referees*. They were the authority in the ring. Even though dad's friends were having a good time, those refs could disqualify people. The in-ring cops in stripes could probably even throw you in jail. Wrestlers backed down from those guys all the time. The biggest, baddest asses in the territory deferred to the referees.

Why was dad still yelling? Is he crazy? We gotta get out of here!

Jason bolted into the locker room to get his stuff and ready himself for the quick exit. He was starting to hyperventilate and the room was getting hazy.

"Goddamn it, Manning! You're full of shit!" Oh God! Dad

won't quit.

Jason was too busy panicking to notice he was standing in the middle of the dressing room, now crying, holding his jacket close to his chest. They were in a world of trouble for sure. They might drag dad away right there. Maybe even take him too.

From the other side of the dressing room, Bruiser Brody, his face a crimson mask awash with blood, saw Jason breaking down. He made his way over and knelt down in front of him. Jason's watery view slowly brought a huge mane of frizzy black hair into focus. Brody's face looked black from the dried blood. He wiped off his blood with both hands.

"Jayce, it's me, Uncle Frank," he said looking into the boy's face. "It's fine. Relax." Jason's breathing slowed a little. He began to calm down and he nodded at Brody.

While Jason knew what his dad and crew did nightly was an agreement, of sorts, he never trusted the referees. Seeing dad and those monsters begging off, working overtime in the ring to deceive the refs was enough to foster a real fear and distrust of them. Let's face it—in the wrestling world, dad was working on the wrong side of the law. If the referee's authority was a shoot, then they were out for dad and probably Jason as well!

What is upside down in a world where dad and his co-workers pretend to beat the shit out of each other and make fans very angry? What would be considered out of the norm? If Gary worked as a babyface manager, the boy's opinion of the policemen of the squared circle would likely have been different. Those refs would have been upholding justice and ensuring that crafty heels and their managers didn't pull the rug out from under dad and his protégé with some illegal tactic. But Gary was a villain and law-and-order was his arch nemesis.

Blurring the lines a little for Jason was also the fact that Gary and David Manning continued this argument well into the backstage area. After Abby and Brody hit the lockers, Gary and Manning stayed in the corridor having it out.

This was a common practice of Gary's and Manning knew to go along with it. The heel manager/booker would always carry whatever happened at ringside well into the rear of the house for fear that an outsider was around. Whether it was an arena maintenance worker, a beat cop, or a local reporter, anyone at the wrestling show would leave believing everything and anything Gary Hart did that night. And David Manning, the consummate pro, went right along with Gary every time. This was an era where believability was everything. Their business didn't exist without it. If Gary wanted to scream at him into the locker room, car, and motel, Manning would go along and give it right back to him.

Jason was adept enough to figure out the work on his own. He resisted asking anyone explicitly. He sensed a question about the validity and truthfulness of his dad's art wouldn't go over big. Wrestling was dad's lifeline.

There were, of course, moments where little droppings of truth would fall out of Gary's mouth.

After Ric Flair lost to Ricky Steamboat in a double arm chicken wing, Jason and Chad were playing around in the pool and using the hold on each other. Gary passed by them.

"Dad," Jason called out. "This doesn't even hurt. We must be doing this wrong."

Gary shook his head as he walked by.

"No, you got it," he said. "Ric lost to a bullshit hold."

SHANE:
Uncle Doink

IF YOUR DAD IS a 400 lb. man with a tattooed head named Bam Bam, then naturally you'd have an Uncle Yoko and an Uncle Doink. You'd always be happy to see the jovial, jolly, 650 lb. Uncle Yoko—the sumo champ Yokozuna, portrayed in real life by a Samoan named Rodney. Doink was an evil clown, of course, and the man under the makeup, Matt Borne, may have been as mischievous as his character. But a wacky, grown man in a full clown outfit that you can call "Uncle" is a blast for a kid to hang with while spending time at dad's job.

When that's the norm, are you really going to ask dad if what was happening in the ring is real? No, you're not. Wrestling was a world that, when ensconced in it, removes any benchmark for reality. What is *real?* What is *fake?* You're hanging with a guy dressed like a clown and a guy the size of a building wearing sumo garb.

Shane Bigelow was yet another child of a wrestler that didn't need to ask about the level of truth in dad's line of work. Like many other kids of that generation, they just figured it out. Perhaps in contrast to the wrestling world of the 1960s or 70s, the wrestling landscape of the 80s and 90s didn't lend itself to much believability. Wrestlers' older kids weren't exactly asking their dads if the evil clown really defeated the garbage man in the ring after distracting him with a midget clown. Actually, *no one* was asking that.

As silly as the WWE locker room was in the mid-90s, an even crazier locker room awaited Bam Bam and his kid in South Philly in the form of ECW. This uncensored and unpredictable federation had a dedicated fan base and its stars were instant cult heroes in 90s wrestling. They were combating a shitty product on WWE and WCW TV, and those were the really big two.

ECW was able to cut through those big two largely due to the danger it put back into wrestling. There was danger in the ring. The workers were pretty dangerous both to themselves and each other. Ringside could be pretty damn dangerous too.

"ECW taught me to be a man," Shane says of the ECW experience. Just being at the shows was implicit permission to be put in several sketchy, dangerous situations per night. "There were more fights in the stands than in the ring."

The ECW locker room was something to contend with as well. It was the land of misfit wrestlers and there were arrests, lunatics, guys with nothing to lose, and lots and lots of drugs. Shane remembers them all as great guys.

"But they were batshit insane," he says.

ECW blurred that believability line for *everyone*. But nothing in the *shoot* or *work* realm had to be explained to Shane, even though plenty of real contact and violence was being served up in ECW. Shane already had a sense of the business pretty well ingrained in him, though. These were still dad's pals—crazy pals, but pals nonetheless.

JJ:
No sling, no foul

HAVING WORKED AS a heel for so many years, JJ Dillon
was a pro at making fans angry. He was a heel manager during
his most successful years as a performer. He managed some of
the more diabolical ring villains like Abdullah the Butcher, Ox
Baker, and Kamala.

But JJ's biggest managerial success came as manager of the
most popular heel faction of all time, The Four Horsemen. The
Horsemen was initially comprised of Ole and Arn Anderson,
Tully Blanchard, and Ric Flair. Replacements would cycle in and
out but this core is considered by many to be the quintessential
line-up.

The Four Horsemen were certainly jeered for their actions
imposed on fan favorites like Dusty Rhodes. But the Four
Horsemen brought something to the bad guy that very few

others had been able to—they were cool. In keeping with the old Hollywood adage which defined the male movie star–women want to be with you and men want to *be* you–The Four Horsemen were as much a draw as any white meat babyface. JJ was their well-appointed, devious mastermind.

By proxy, lots of that Horseman cool rubbed off on JJ. He didn't portray a sniveling mama's boy or a maniacal mouth breather. He didn't evoke the desire to smack the shit out of him. He was one to outwit. He was clever and carried himself a class beyond the average wrestling fan.

But he was an exception to a fact of life for those who worked the black hat during the era of kayfabe—fans would sometimes try the heels in public. JJ didn't have problems when he was out. His kids didn't see him harassed and he didn't really need to have a discussion with them about what daddy did being theatre.

It is likely the character of JJ Dillon that kept fans in line when coming across him in the streets. He treated fans with respect, whether cheering him or jeering him. That's the key to keeping away from punches. The kids always saw JJ and the fans engaging in a dance of that mutual respect. They didn't have reason to fear, so they didn't.

In JJ's tenure with both WCW and WWE he spent much of that time in the federations' offices, working behind the scenes. JJ's children were always around the tedious, business aspect of wrestling as well as what was going on in the ring. Of course they'd seen JJ on TV, but it was always counter-balanced with wrestlers just being around. As a result, he never really had a need to smarten up his children.

"From the very beginning I was working the office and around the business, talent would come and go," JJ said. "They'd always seen me on television, so it was never a big deal." They never looked at it like he was a celebrity.

"I guess they realized I came home every night, and regardless of what they saw on television, I came home without an ambulance and without my arm in a sling. So it was never a big deal."

KEVIN:
Forgive me father

A DEVIL AND A prophet stood on the steps of a church. What sounds like the opening of a joke was an actual Sunday morning in Tampa. It was every Sunday morning, actually. The Sullivan kids, Ben and Shannon, were dutifully brought to their local church every Sunday by their Irish Catholic, wrestler father. Some weeks Kevin, knowledgeable in philosophy and religions of the world, would stand and chat with the local priest.

An odd, troubling sight for some parishioners who were fans of the sport.

The early 1980s brought with it a commitment to the believability of the wresting product. Kevin believed in that code because in it lived the artery of his livelihood. Kevin, as a heel, thrived on the believability of a character he created, and the terror and havoc it created. He was a prominent figure on Florida wresting TV, so one might think it odd if they ran into him having a chat with the local priest on the church steps.

If you watched Championship Wrestling from Florida in the 1980s, you feared Kevin Sullivan. Kevin's heel actions on TV were tinged more than a little bit with undertones of the occult and a dark, mystical underworld. Kevin and his cabal of fiends were violent. They decorated their faces with symbols drawn in black paint. They wore hooded robes, like druids or worse.

Kevin, ever-wise in his construction of the bad guy persona, knew he had to human to be feared. He was announced nightly as "Kevin Sullivan." He didn't wrestle as The Warlock or The Red Death, as would be the knee-jerk temptation of a booker less skilled and more disrespectful of an audience than he. He was Kevin Sullivan—fully human, walking among the people, we assumed, in his daily life. But within him lay a darkness, conjured by practices that happened under moonlight, maybe even involved the letting of blood.

Man, did Kevin know our imaginations were far worse than any special effect he could perform in the ring.

So when Kevin brought the kids to mass in Tampa on Sundays, it was inevitable that the priest would broach the topic. And he did so with a wisdom and insight that surprised and pleased Kevin.

"You're doing a role, like Dr. Jekyll and Mr. Hyde," the priest began. "You do it pretty well, but if people want to believe in this stuff, there's something wrong in *them*."

Kevin also did something, or better said, *didn't* do

something, that was subtle but didn't go unnoticed by the priest.

"You're smart not to come right out and say the word 'devil,'" the father said. He was right. And Kevin knew why.

"The Catholic church kind of dances around exorcism pretty easily," Kevin said. "Now, they'll say it's mostly people that are bipolar, or have problems. They won't come out and say demonic possession." Kevin draws a comparison on how he protected his illusion, and how the church handled one of its more controversial practices. If either started throwing more definitive words around, they ran the risk of ridicule.

Keep it mystical, keep it vague. We fear the unknown anyway. Grown-ups do.

For the Sullivan kids, there was no reason to ask certain questions about believability. Kids of that generation, as we are learning in this study, did a lot of work on their own. They weren't afraid to probe the unknown and come to some conclusion for themselves. Did they need to ask anything of an Irish Catholic dad who drove them to mass on Sundays but donned a cloak and face paint for work at night? They didn't need to utter words like 'real' and 'fake.'

"Kids could see through it and adults couldn't," Sullivan says. Shannon and Ben also had the benefit of seeing it from the home. They might see their father bleeding from the head on TV, wearing a bandage on his forehead for two weeks' worth of interviews. Then he would come home from work at night and the Band Aid would come off. Before heading out the next day, a Band Aid would go on.

"They figured it out pretty quick," he says. "Sometimes we don't give credit to kids for being smart enough and their mind opening. They don't have anything written on the slate yet. They're willing to look at something they've never seen before and figure it out."

In the 80s when Kevin was working in Florida, the kids would hear Kevin on the phone in the house. They were around the creative aspect of wrestling's illusion as Kevin was making decisions, but it just didn't seem noteworthy to them. They weren't fans of the sport, and they didn't pause in their activities at home long enough to care about what these discussions of snakes and Abudadein were. As Kevin put it, those discussion just "rolled off their backs."

Smartening up was more common sense than overhearing discussions on booking. They saw dad leave the house, they saw dad come home. "He got elbowed in the head by Dusty, he hit him in the face, and his face looks like it did when he left the house," Kevin says of his kids' observations.

Another prime example of the kids' detective work doing the smartening was the matter of those little slips of paper on the kitchen table. The kids saw Sullivan feuding with Mike Graham, promoter Eddie's Graham's son. They were having bloody battles all over the Sunshine State. Yet, there on the table sat paychecks for hundreds and hundreds of dollars, all signed by Eddie Graham.

He's paying dad to beat up his son?

Kevin wonders how more people didn't pick up on that. He continued to do heinous things, warranting suspension or worse, to the promoter's son and he was allowed to continue working and get paid by Eddie's promotion. It sure tipped off his kids.

But what about the contest? Wrestling is sport, is it not? There's a winner and a loser. Kevin assumes the kids may have thought some of the moves were real, but he's fairly certain they knew the finishes were choreographed, winners predetermined.

The kids came out to the matches for fun. The adults came out for blood, and they'd try and get a swing in themselves if the babyface couldn't do it for them. How myopic we become when we "mature" and shed the need for fun.

It is easy to assume the revelatory discussion Lanny Poffo had with Magen about the work he was doing on TV happened in every wrestler's living room at some point in their kids' lives. One would think it was the wrestler's duty to smarten up the kids, allaying their fears for dad's well being in the ring. Enough of that old-world, kayfabe bullshit, now. These are their kids we're talking about here.

That assumption would be wrong. Of the talent profiled, it was actually *only* Lanny that had that talk. It was a spontaneous thing. Lanny hadn't rehearsed for the day he'd need to break Magen of the pacifier of kayfabe. She was watching him on TV, getting upset, and not able to grasp the whole illusion as he stood in the very room in which she was watching him get his ass kicked. He stepped in and did the thing dads do—repair things that crumble around our kids.

The other wrestlers didn't avoid discussions of illusion and work because of a blood oath or any allegiance to history. The kids were near dad, near the business of wrestling, and they connected the dots. Had Magen not had that discussion as a toddler, she would have done that work on her own as well. It's what kids do—they figure shit out. They know where the Christmas presents are. And if they don't, they just haven't tried.

That was the single element of this journey that may be most shocking to the layperson—wrestling families didn't need to have that discussion, didn't need to work out some code of ethics for the children of the magician.

"You know, daddy makes things look one way for most people, and another way for you. If people ask you about it, you just let them see it the way I make them see it. And you can see it another way."

So intriguing and mysterious would such discussions be— how Kevin Sullivan sat the kids down and explained how he and Vincent Price were kinda the same. That would have been great, but the kids just didn't need it. Almost none of them did.

And why should anyone have thought they would have needed it? We watched what they did as a kid—far less of it than the kid of a worker—and no one had to sit me down and explain anything to me. From very early on I saw the glint in the eye of every worker.

I sat in arenas, waited in the rain for autographs from these guys. I saw them up close, the heels too. I saw how scary Bundy, Afa and Sika, and Studd were when they walked past me. But I don't think I was afraid of them.

In awe? For certain. But I always felt they were there at that arena *for* me. Damn, if one of them lived in my home, I would have known much more, much sooner.

We figured it out, guys. Remember?

4.

THE SCHOOL YEARS

I DON'T THINK I ever feared my mother or the physical punishments she attempted to deliver. I could be a real prick as a youngster and once my father was out of the picture, that element of fear was eliminated from consequence. Yeah, I might get grounded again. Might have to endure her crow-like squawking she thought deterred, rather than irritated.

How might those pre-teen years have differed if I had someone who gouged another man's head until it drew blood that night, returning home to discipline me? *"Wait until your father gets home"* pales beside *"Wait until your 300 pound, scarred, injured heel father gets home after his dog collar match tonight."*

Childhood is a rollercoaster of moments that warrant such

threats, and also moments of pride and life affirming lessons. Parents endure the pain of disciplinary responsibilities with the promise of getting to the finish line, which might be the graduation, ballet recital, or the big football game. If we are thankful for missing the prior, we are devastated missing the latter.

Though the wresting dad has some latitude with certain aspects of home life, there is one undeniable truth, and that is the amount of time they will be away from the children and the home. That has ramifications in all facets of the household, for the wife and also the kids.

The challenge, and the gradient of success, is determined by the degree of normalcy that is needed for all. Kids are pretty adaptable—normal is whatever their life is. That's the bar that gets set. If it's handled responsibly by the wrestling dad and his wife, it's a shorter path to normal, cage matches and bloodstained shirts aside. That responsible handing of a family structure in a very atypical world is not as easy as it rolls off the tongue. It can be a Herculean task.

Far too often in the frontier land that was the wrestling world, the workers could not help but sabotage themselves and all in their path. Some wreaked havoc on themselves from both a business and personal standpoint. Many introduced that havoc into their personal lives. As we discussed, it was not an industry that fostered the best of decisions.

ERIC:
Higher education

FATE HAD ALWAYS guided Eric Bischoff along pretty gracefully. But fate usually looks to partner with work ethic in creating a marriage of fortuitous events, and Eric had that work ethic in abundance.

There's always a guy in the office, any office, that's never at his cubicle because he's buzzing round the building. He's talking to everyone, trying to overhear everything. He's been there a week and he already knows the names of every executive and each of their administrative assistants. He's shaken their hands in the elevator, brought their admins a latte on the way to his lowly, first-floor cubicle. He leaves late, even if it means arranging the paper clips in the drawer, so the dude in the corner office can see him still there.

He's a man with a plan, and that scares the other cubicle

dwellers. They become distrustful of him, sensing he might push them out a window to gain another rung on the corporate ladder. And he might.

The higher-ups know that pesky guy's name too. And in a pinch they might need to tell their assistant to grab a guy off the floor who can organize his paper clips. Or maybe they *need* someone pushed out a window.

"Bob, what's that fucking kid's name—the one with the really white teeth smiling at my secretary all the time?"

"Oh, yeah…Eric-Something. Gave me an autographed football for Christmas, didn't even know his name."

"Have him come into the meeting later. Need a pair of fresh eyes from the floor to look at this. He's always running around here, full of ideas."

What no one knows is that little guy took his prized, Joe Namath-signed ball off his shelf at home before going into work on December 23rd.

Eric Bischoff is that kind of guy. Imagine trying to straddle both the carnival world of pro wrestling and big business? What qualities would you pour into that stew as you stood in a human laboratory? They resemble someone, no?

Eric was flying back and forth between Atlanta and Minneapolis for about a year before it had really become just too much. When he was splitting the week between home and WCW that was one thing—everyone at home could get used to three or four days on, three days off. But as his responsibility grew and he was flying home late Friday, sleeping Saturday, and heading back to Atlanta on Sunday night, his schedule simply cut his family off too aggressively.

But what the hell do you do? He was rising in the ranks of this massive, entertainment entity, making real money, and building that moat around his family that financial stability can.

Just as Eric felt his breaking point approaching, fate took the hand of that diligent guy running around CNN Center. In the summer of 1993, a Turner executive came to Eric and pointed out they were paying significant money shuttling Eric back and forth every week. It would make more sense if they dropped a few bucks and just moved his family out in one fell swoop. Then his commutes to the studio shows would be local.

It was a great deal. Eric was basically working 9-6, with the occasional overnight for a pay-per-view. But for the most part it was a day job. Now Loree and the kids would be a commute away, every day. He jumped at it. Loree was her customary supportive self, agreeing to uproot the family and head to Atlanta despite her own family roots in Minnesota.

They put their home on the market back in Minneapolis and made a call to Dusty Rhodes's wife Michelle, a real estate agent in Atlanta. Eric had been working closely with Dusty since going to WCW. Dusty kept Eric close, making sure he learned the landscape in the proper way and understood everything they were doing. He got Michelle on the case, looking for a place outside Atlanta.

Coincidentally, a home became available on the same street where Michelle just sold Diamond Dallas Page and his wife a house. Loree went to see it, not even knowing DDP or that the Pages were living a couple of doors away. The Bischoffs were soon neighbors with the Pages. After bouncing around for a couple of years, Eric's schedule stabilized greatly, as did his home life. He was seeing Garett and Montanna daily. He eased into that new, placid reality which would last for a couple of years.

Things got pretty intense for Eric in late 1995. A ton of responsibility had been dropped in his lap. He was out traveling with Nitro and found himself away from Atlanta four and five days a week. He was feeling the pangs of a familiar pain, being away from family more than he would have liked. His and Loree's relationship was solid and that was the foundation that allowed Eric to keep a stable home, despite the demands of the road.

Eric compensated for those travel demands as best he could for the next few years, as his Nitro product became the crown jewel in WCW's programming, and the first real threat to

WWE's undisputed romp through the business for ten years. When WCW was shooting syndicated TV at Disney's MGM Studios, Eric made it a point to bring the family down. When Eric would head to Japan for meetings, he took them.

Eric's kids were no different from the children of wrestlers, having to cope with their dad's extended absences and an over-reliance on mom. However there *was* significant difference in dad's ability to offset some of that when dad was President of the company.

When Eric felt he was away from the kids for too long, he would simply sign them out of school and take them with him. He was a licensed pilot and had his own plane at the time, so he could throw them in there and fly them off to wherever business was taking him. Decimals and square roots are great and all, but they were learning something much more unique and advanced by traveling with Eric. They had the rare opportunity to see the world and witness the machinations of big business.

Make no mistake, Garett's and Montanna's time beside their father during his business-changing tenure at the helm of WCW was higher education at its finest.

As Nitro exploded, Eric was spending a great deal of time on-camera, doing his best to be a total asshole. As we've seen here, he certainly wasn't the first heel to have kids. Many kids had to go into school and prepare to discuss, or ignore, reactions to what their dad did on TV.

But the kind of heel Eric was creating, both for himself as well as the wrestlers in his NWO stable, were game changing. These bad guys were of the Tarantino mold—slick tongued, black-clad, and cooler than the fan faves. Do you want to be the kid cheering for face paint when the arena is popping for black leather?

And therein lies the seismic shift in the business that changed it forever—the image of the babyface was reborn. It was wrestling 2.0, without a doubt. It's been called the *Monday Night Wars* and similar monikers, but it was the great storm that reshaped the terrain. Between ECW, the NWO, and WWE's Attitude branding, those years were the modern day renaissance for the sport.

Even if the kids at school believed what they saw on TV on Monday nights to be reality, Garett's dad was cool as shit for being a badass. Garett's dad saw to it that playing that bad guy card the right way in 1996 would make you cool as shit.

Of course, off-camera Eric was the regular guy on the block. He wasn't particularly badass, and certainly wasn't living the lifestyle of the rogue wild men wearing the NWO black and white in the ring. He was still the boss and was very aware of the weight of his responsibilities to the company that began to actually beat WWE in the ratings.

Bischoff's position as President certainly benefitted Loree and the kids in the obvious ways—bringing them to Disney if they were apart for too long, or flying the kids away with him in a personal plane. But his executive position also insulated him from the more subtle pitfalls of the road that destroyed workers' homes. The road was different for the boss.

Simply put, *everything* was different for the boss.

"I wasn't a wrestler," Eric began. "I didn't live a wrestler's lifestyle. I'd be up at 5:30 a.m., getting into a limo to fly to the Atlanta airport to fly to New York or LA for business meetings. I wasn't on the road with three or four other guys drinking beers and smoking a joint trying to get to the next town."

The discipline required to run the $300 million dollar operation that WCW had become placed Bischoff in a pen. Around him, beasts ran wild and unchained. There was too much to do in the wire cage. He couldn't fuck-off if he wanted to. The position of President benefitted both his family and his well being.

"Humans have flaws," Eric said. "Shit happens on the road. Opportunities to do stupid things happen on the road."

The lifestyle of the executive on the road greatly limited the chances to make bad choices. Exposing his family to the business and including them in the lifestyle benefitted all of them.

"Had I been wrestler I probably wouldn't have wanted them around [the business]." But being an executive was different.

Reflecting on the journey from imitation crab meat to an office in CNN Center can be daunting. The biggest change in Loree and Eric was in their view of business, from micro to macro. Decisions were no longer centered around a small, local product. It was big business. They were in it together, as they had been from Day One. They made their kids a part of it too.

Eric can trace the Bischoff's strong family bond back to Loree's steadfast willingness to support anything that would benefit her family. Like when Bill Shaw first said he was looking to hire an Executive Producer to resurrect WCW after its precipitous fall under Bill Watts's direction.

"There's nobody on the planet better than you to take that job," she said to him.

"I don't know if that's true," Eric replied, "but I'm going with that."

LANNY:
Check, please

"I ONLY STAYED married because I was a Catholic," Lanny Poffo said. Though his marriage to Sally was beginning to fall apart, Lanny found safe haven in the arms of denial and the fortification of staunch, Catholic values espoused by Angelo. But realistically, you can't work on saving a marriage during a time before cell phones, communication limited to calls from pay phones and hotel room phones, with the travel schedule Lanny had in the 80s.

The degree to which one might attribute responsibility for marriages' dissolutions to the absence from the home varies. Some made it work—no doubt the product of inhuman tolerance on the part of the wives.

Second-generation workers like Lanny saw travel demands firsthand as a child, though the wives didn't have that. As much as one can imagine or plan for a spouse's foray into a high profile, pro wrestling spotlight, the day-to-day reality of such is different. And once everyone wakes up and smells the coffee, the hard work begins.

However, the WWE's taxing travel schedule wasn't so much an issue for young Magen. The girl missed her daddy, no question. But Lanny was always conscious of the potential toll it was taking on her. When he would return home from a long stretch of road dates, Lanny always marked the occasion with presents for her. Admittedly, he was guilty of trying to buy the girl's love.

There wasn't any reason for Lanny *not* to have Magen's love, and she was a rather remarkable little lady, never invoking the "daddy is gone too much" card. It was more Lanny's guilt from having been gone so much. Magen was used to Lanny's extended road trips for the national federation. Either through her overly mature nature or Lanny's efforts to compensate, the gift of a dad and daughter's bond always remained.

Lanny's awareness and attention paid to the needs of a child of a wresting star was uncanny in the business. Not to be overlooked as a reason for this is Lanny's youth, having been locked between Angelo, star of the ring, and Randy, star of the baseball diamond. He himself no doubt spent years wondering where he fit.

He would not take chances with Magen. He would ensure Magen knew that her place was firmly in his heart.

Workers on the road were at the mercy of their promoter's itinerary, but when there were gaps in that schedule it was opportunity to make up for lost time with family. When Lanny was home he'd make that time count, in what's become a welcomed theme for many in this study. Lanny tried to do the things parents who weren't being flattened by King Kong Bundy for twenty-five days a month did, like help out at Magen's school. But Lanny's celebrity status allowed him to take it further than most. He would speak at Magen's school, guest lecturing about the dangers of drugs.

What neither she nor her classmates knew was that Lanny had begun using Deca-Durabolin—an intramuscular, injectable steroid. As his TV time began to increase during his run as the villainous character "The Genius," which included a spot against Hulk Hogan on NBC's *Saturday Night's Main Event*, he began using Deca to get physically bigger. Some sort of chemical enhancement was a near necessity in his line of work for that time period. Without size, you'd be lost among the monsters getting all the airtime. That meant less of a push, less work, less money, and maybe no job—no doubt a conundrum for anyone balancing a family and an ethical high ground.

Steroids helped keep many a worker gainfully employed. But it was illegal and also unhealthy. It was a moral compromise as Lanny stood before students and told the room to "say no."

Though Sally's and Lanny's marriage became more untenable, the religion thing was still doing a number on Lanny. He knew the union wasn't working but those Catholic instincts, instilled fiercely, reminded him that bailing wasn't an option that would be looked upon favorably by either the Holy Father or the Poffo father. Angelo was still a figure looming large over

Lanny.

Also, no small consideration was Magen. Ultimately, Lanny also felt a duty to keep the nuclear family together until she was older. He felt there were valid reasons for leaving, but ultimately the forces that made him stay were far stronger. He tried to make the best of it and focused wholeheartedly on his daughter.

Lanny's positivity is a remarkable trait. He doesn't blame wrestling for the marriage failing. One could cite the number of consecutive dates he worked at his peak, the hours away from home. And though he'd agree that the nature of the wrestler's lifestyle has a host of poisonous tentacles, he believes none of them did any more harm than could have been done in any other industry. That's his perspective on it.

Lanny is quick to point out that lots of college graduates with 9 to 5 jobs are divorced. It ain't just those wrestlers with their rats and road stories. He thinks about that.

"Seems I don't know anyone that *isn't* divorced."

Lanny Poffo is a guy that is reluctant to cast blame anyway. He's a rugged individualist at heart—taking full responsibility for his foibles and deeply relishing the spoils of his good decisions. He blames no one, but owes no one.

In 2002, when their daughter graduated high school, Sally and Lanny ended their marriage. He'd already been in it longer than he should have, perhaps for the right reasons. But he now felt his daughter was in a better place to deal with the news. And *he* was in a better place to divorce himself from the dogmatic constraints that religion placed on him.

"There's three things a Catholic doesn't do—divorce, abortion, and suicide," Lanny said. "And now that I'm divorced, I'm curious about abortion and suicide."

SHANE:
After the pills

SHANE BIGELOW WAS waiting at a red light and kept checking the rearview mirror. His heart was fluttering, his hands clammy. He was going to be in a world of shit if he got popped by a cop.

He shouldn't have been driving and he knew that, of course. He was very careful—going slowly and eyeing that white line like it was holding him to the earth. The car wasn't his, taken very much without permission, and he was very much only 15 years-old. All of this, very much against the law.

Sitting at that red light and reflecting back to the course of events that brought him here could have rattled the youngster ever more. So he tried to stay focused, just drive, accomplish his mission, and get back. He blocked out the memories of younger years with his father and the sheer idolatry he had for the giant that made *him* feel like a giant. Those were great days.

Then, like happened to so many families, divorce entered the picture.

For all of what Bam Bam was to Shane in his youngest years, he'd morphed into a man so unlike that in the short time following the split with his wife. The divorce of Bam Bam and Shane's mom was a tipping point.

"I got a lot of harsh lessons when my parents split up," Shane said. In the 8ᵗth grade, Shane's life took the turn that millions of American children's lives do. All these kids have to learn to now live with a mother and father that have acknowledged to the world, and most painfully to them, that living without the other parent is the best thing. It's counterintuitive to all that has been fostered in the child's psyche for years prior, with both parents in the home. Even if things weren't perfect, there were still roles in that home, and a mom and a dad filled them.

But now that thing that happens to all those other kids' parents takes over the dynamic of one's own home. And now it's reality.

The reality of the divorce of Shane's parents was crude. It was not amicable and in the process of splitting up, Shane's mom and dad aired each others' dirty laundry. The results of hearing his parents' passionate displeasure for one another was emotionally damaging to Shane. To him, Bam Bam was still the heroic figure he'd see on TV, and then rush to the airport to greet. Admittedly, and not properly, Shane chose a side in the split. And it was dad's side.

Eventually he went to live with Bam Bam. Shane's positioning himself with his dad, across the red line in the sand from his mom, caused tension between mother and son. It was a sacrifice he was willing to make—though he was likely too young to be judicious about such a thing—to be with his father during the turmoil.

Shane was not prepared for much of what began happening when he moved in with his father. Bam Bam's body was deteriorating from the years of impact endured by the high-flying, 300 pounder's ring work. Shane was there with his father and saw the 43 year-old man's half-hour process to get out of bed in the morning. The bodily abuse from years in the ring had accumulated exponentially.

Years before the divorce, there were times when Bam Bam would change his flight to an earlier time so he could stop at Monmouth Medical Center to get stitches before seeing his family without telling his wife. His body was riddled with bone spurs and stenosis and he was so very often in pain. Bam Bam's need for prescription painkillers was as valid as any case a doctor could have seen hobble into the office.

There was no professional athlete that didn't know the possibility of painkiller dependence and its dangers. All of us common folk know it as well, and we roll the dice for a root canal. Walking in a body shattered to smithereens for twenty years yields a desperation for relief that is beyond the day worker's comprehension.

The invitation to heal the chronic pain with prescribed painkillers is an open door in the storm. The conditions outside are horrendous and who on earth wouldn't want to step inside and warm up? The pills could give your life back. They can make you who you should be, who you once were before life was compromised.

They are a dark, dark gift.

Walking in through that open door puts one in an unpredictable place. How one reacts to being inside is as individual as the person. There are a host of variables. Can you live within the limits of just your prescription? If you can't, will you go through proper channels to handle that? As a professional wrestler, or former pro wrestler, your pain isn't going away. Can you deal with that?

A dark side emerged as Bam Bam began relying more and more heavily on pills to survive. Whereas at one time Shane would go fishing with his dad, Bam Bam was now often too out of it. There was a sadness in Bam Bam when he'd have to reject Shane's requests for a hunting excursion or the like. It killed him that he couldn't do that stuff anymore, and Shane saw it in his eyes when he'd take a pass on spending time with his boy. Bam Bam's body had already been broken and now the pills were breaking his spirit. Slowly, watching it all began to break something in Shane. He was heartbroken.

The kid was no idiot. Even as an early teenager, he knew not everyone had the best interests in mind for his dad, and that included people that had always been considered friends. As Bam Bam became more isolated from his brothers in the wrestling business, other people steered themselves more prominently into his life.

There was a doctor friend of Bam Bam's that always seemed to be his biggest fan and best friend. But once Bam Bam was out on his own, he likely became something else. So often people cannot see an addiction festering in someone close to them. They see the pain in their friend's eyes. They see them struggle to walk and sit. Maybe they block the risks out in their desire to heal their friend. But that other stuff is real, those risks. Common sense, it seems, should have intervened, particularly for a physician.

"You've got a guy who's a doctor," Shane says. "He's revered in the community, coming over to your house smiling. He's your father's best friend, touting him all over town. Then, eventually the road takes its toll [on Bam Bam] and this guy has no right writing prescriptions and he's unloading them left and right, polluting the person you grew up with." Shane stood-by in disgust, young but knowing.

That afternoon in the stolen car, 15 year-old Shane would make it home just fine. He was only out for a little while, long enough to grab some food. He wasn't exactly the joyriding type. He wasn't the stealing-a-car type either.

The stolen car was Bam Bam's. Shane once again found himself, and this time his little 3 year-old sister, alone with a completely incapacitated father. Attempts to rouse him were futile. The little girl was hungry and there was no food around. More and more, there seemed to be less and less of *everything* around. There were once Corvettes, motorcycles, and a bunch of great quality fishing rods around. They were disappearing. Shane's mother would soon get wind of everything being liquidated and get Shane back home before the bottom fell out completely. She saw her son was standing beside someone he loved, but on a sinking ship. And that afternoon driving his dad's car, Shane heard the faint echoes of reason illustrating that.

It was getting late and the baby had to eat. Shane would sneak out and take Bam Bam's car, say a prayer, and try and get some grub. As far as low points go, Shane knew he was below sea level with this scenario. The man who was once ten feel tall in a world of pygmies, couldn't even stand. He couldn't provide food in the house for his children. He was done, in every sense. He was fading from the tangible world and, tragically, in the eyes of the boy who once looked at him like a God.

Scott "Bam Bam" Bigelow, the legend of Monmouth County, was evaporating.

VINCE:
TV or not TV

THE CHILD OF A heel wrestler in the kayfabe era could expect some guff, if not friendly joshing, from the neighborhood kids. A schoolyard comment or two was probably not unlikely when your dad was unleashing dastardly and devious tactics on television every week. But as we've seen here, kids are figuring out a lot of what's happening on-camera on their own. They've made a psychological peace with what's portrayed as evil on television, in pro wrestling.

Something unprecedented started to happen to pro wrestling in the 1990s. Fans began to not only know and accept the sport as illusion, but there were available media outlets that openly discussed the tricks, the trade, and the offstage lives of the magicians. The Internet explosion offered the wrestling fan a host of websites that would report what was previously only available to those that knew about wrestling "dirt sheet" newsletters, and only in locker rooms before that.

Suddenly, the Tuesday morning water cooler discussions about wrestling were that of quarter-hour ratings and talent contracts, and no longer run-ins and chair shots. It was more important to a large segment of fans when someone bumped a rating than how they bumped in the ring. The story telling was gone. The guys telling the story, *became* the story.

So too did the guys behind the telling of the stories. Vince Russo, head writer, became the subject of discussion on wrestling's first Internet radio shows (the term podcast had yet to be coined) aired on outlets like EYADA. The ratings war between WWE and WCW was being covered in publications like *The Wrestling Observer* and *The Pro Wrestling Torch*, the two most popular purveyors of wrestling's insider news. So guys like McMahon, Russo, and Bischoff were being spoken about by name, their decisions critiqued after the fact and, at times, revealed before the fact.

So when exactly did the world start to hate Vince Russo?

I can tell you everyone hated Larry Zbyszko when he hit his beloved mentor Bruno Sammartino with a chair on TV in 1980. I can tell you Shawn Michaels kicked his brother-in-arms Marty Jannetty through a glass window on TV, turning fans passionately against him.

But Russo was a writer. He would later put himself on TV as a character in the shows, then get into a wrestling ring himself—heresy for the purist. But even before he was in the ring, his writing was being critiqued by the masses thanks to this new look inside the business. Russo's TV product was on the cusp of indecency at times, and just plain silly other times. It drove ratings, and drove wrestling purists nuts.

Russo's sons (Annie was too young) might now be privy to fan hate of their dad. Not a character, not a fabrication of a booker's mind, but their real father. But remarkably, likely due to the fact that wrestling websites and newsletters were not finding the 12 year-old crowd, Will and V.J. never reported issues to their parents.

See, the Russo boys were never fans of the sport. Imagine having access to "Stone Cold" Steve Austin and The Rock in person and the ability to hang out at WWE TV tapings, and never wanting to. The kids just didn't get the allure of wrestling.

Besides, their dad was now working for some company in Atlanta called WCW. One good thing Russo did by jumping over to the WWE's rival company was loosen his schedule a bit. As a specific part of this contract with WCW, it was not mandatory that Russo be in attendance for every taping. If he didn't want to go to TV that week, he didn't have to. If he felt his family was being neglected due to his being out with WCW too much, he could stay home and let his assistant, Ed Ferrara, run things. The TV script was written already.

When Vince McMahon dismissed Russo's desire to be around his family more, Russo decided he was walking. When he inked an agreement with WCW, it was imperative he not be made prisoner, and he put all the verbiage in his contract that would see to that—most notably his not having to attend TV tapings in person.

Those provisions would only be relevant for about three months before political struggles began to consume the creative direction of the company. Russo was soon home, languishing in the house with full pay for nearly six months. At that point he was called back to work for another six month run before the company's demise entirely.

During that time, Russo and his family would be out at a restaurant and he'd get noticed by fans because he was on-camera. But his kids didn't really bother taking notice. They weren't aware of what he was doing on TV so they really didn't get the big deal.

Russo made it a point to be with the kids 24/7 now, whenever he was home. He very rarely brought them around the wrestling business and did everything in his power to keep the two worlds separate. Once in a blue moon they'd come to a TV taping and they attended the Fan Fest at Wrestlemania X. He was falling out of love with it anyway, and the jury is still out as to whether there was anything he ever loved about it in the first place.

TITO:
The pee game

TITO SANTANA WALKED into the door of his New Jersey home after not seeing the inside of it for the past 12 days. His wife, Leah, and his 3 boys were home and for days he'd been thinking of nothing but seeing their faces. The WWE was in its heyday, having packed 93,000 fans into the Pontiac Silverdome for the record breaking pay-per-view Wrestlemania III.

Tito was still a dependable name for the massive wrestling company and he was cranking out over 300 dates a year, crisscrossing the country. WWE maintained a heavy concentration of dates in the Northeast so by keeping a home in New Jersey, he was able to be home more than some of the guys that lived in Florida or Georgia. When WWE ran Boston, Philadelphia, Landover, Baltimore, and New York City, he could drive those shots and be home. Tito tried to keep about a

300 mile radius around his home that he would consider a road trip. He'd opt to drive rather than fly so he could wake up with Leah and the kids.

Yet there were still times when his loop was out west or hitting spot shows in the Midwest. He could be gone for seven, eight, ten days—a web of flights, rental cars, hotels keeping him from home.

Walking into that door after being away for 12 days, he was desperate for some attention from the wife and overall fanfare from the family. That's what he *expected*. What he got was reality—an exhausted wife and busy home. Leah was home alone with the kids all the time. Many times she was both mom and dad.

Tito would jump right in and play with the kids and take over when he got in the door. But there was a reality to that too. Tito was exhausted from his road schedule, and he'd be pulled back out the door a day or so later. It was an endless grind, and was being felt by both the road-weary Tito and home-weary Leah.

The perfect solution came in the form of a nanny. Tito's idea, not Vince McMahon's. In one fell swoop Tito solved much of the strife that his impossible schedule created for his home. Their nanny worked well and would up with them for seven years.

As for the boys, dad's absences were mitigated by having a father in the spotlight in 1980's WWE. The sport's overwhelming popularity and the fact that Tito was a beloved babyface made the boys popular. They had the biggest house of all their friends and it was the hang-out spot. When pay-per-views were on, all the kids got together at Tito's house. It was cool to be friends with Tito's boys.

With kayfabe largely dead and the emphasis on protecting the illusion of the sport no longer enforced, the kids didn't get grief from the other kids. And Tito never had to explain anything about the illusion, either. They watched, and they figured it all out.

"I never really had to smarten my kids up," he said. "They smartened themselves up."

It would have been impossible for them not to have known pro wrestling was show, given the environment of a WWE locker room in the late 80s and 90s. When Tito did the shots where he could drive, he would bring all three kids as they loved the shows and it offered Tito that precious time together. Wherever he could combine work with family time, he did.

The boys would pile into the minivan for the road trips with their dad and their empty milk container. The container was part of a game the boys devised wherein they would measure the distance of the trip by how much urine they could collectively fill the carton with. This was clearly a household raising only boys.

At the arenas, the kids enjoyed hanging with all the workers. Wrestling locker rooms were a true fraternity. When Tito would head to the ring, one of the other workers would offer to watch the kids. Heels and babyfaces alike would help out and hang with them for the duration of the match. There's hardly a need to smarten up anyone who is being babysat by the guy that's facing their dad in a steel cage match in Baltimore tomorrow night.

After the card, they'd all get back in the minivan and Tito would let the kids choose the fast food drive thru for the ride back. They'd eat and the kids would be asleep by the time they hit I-95.

"It was a fun time for me, hanging out with them."

Tito's family is still in tact today. He is still married to Leah and maintains close relationships with his sons, all in their 30s as of this writing. Tito's parents were divorced when he was a sophomore in college and even at that age it affected him greatly.

"It left a scar in my life," he said. "I swore to myself, my kids were never going to experience that. I made a commitment—I wanted to be married *once*."

Tito said his family was always first, and it's easy to chalk that up as lip service or an easy catchphrase. But Tito lived it. There's a reason he has kept a happy home for 40 years and survived the carnival that is pro wrestling. By all accounts, he's normal. His family is normal. They are the ultra-rare familial success story in the business.

Tito thinks there's a very clear reason for that.

"You gotta have a woman next to you that feels the same way. Things happen in a relationship, and I was lucky that I had a very strong relationship with my wife and my kids, and we're still together."

KEVIN:
In the bubble

SHANNON AND BEN Sullivan's formative years were spent in Tampa during Kevin's tenure with Championship Wrestling from Florida. They spent their early school years watching dad conjure up ancient spells and other confusing, disjointed mysticism while stomping the tar out of blonde-haired babyfaces. Having already studied the charade and accepted the above as more theatre than anything else, the kids went about their normal 7 and 8 year-old activities with their friends. Surprisingly, they weren't subjected to teasing or questions about why daddy had a black "X" grease painted on his forehead.

Workers in the Florida territory in the early and mid 80s followed a housing ritual that became the norm for wrestlers and their families coming to the region. Tampa was a growing city at the time and there were apartment complexes popping up all over the city.

And some of those were babyface complexes, and some were heel complexes.

Eddie Graham was a promoter legendary for his fierceness in protecting the illusion of kayfabe—the legitimacy of the wrestling business and all it portrayed. Babyfaces and heels were never to be seen fraternizing. In the days before cell phone cameras in everyone's holster, you could do this. If you were careful.

Years before Kevin got there, Johnny Valentine and Red Bastein were the two marquee names feuding in Championship Wrestling from Florida and making scores of cash for the federation and its owner, Eddie Graham. Rivals in the ring and on TV, they were doing it all right.

Off-camera, not so much.

The two wresters with a thirst for each other's blood made a critical error in the kayfabe era—they were seen together. All of this is likely taken with a grain of salt and looked at with a shrug these days, but the death of the illusion was the death of the business back then. Wrestlers were seen as warriors, not actors. Most of the workers were careful with this and the smarter-than-average fan played along, gloriously suspending any whispering of disbelief. It was a rip-roaring, fun night at the matches.

Get him, Red!

Promoter Eddie Graham was approached by a fan who reported living beside one of "your wrestlers" in an apartment near the beach. One afternoon, tucked in the rear of an apartment backyard, the fan saw Red Bastein and Johnny Valentine having a drink at the *same barbecue.*

Eddie seethed. At risk was not just that illusion they all worked so hard to create, but Eddie's gate and company. He did the hardest thing possible, the *only* thing that could underscore the severity of the infraction—he fired his two highest profile stars, right in the middle of their feud.

The reverberations of that punishment shook up wrestlers in the Florida territory for years. A practice was developed in Tampa wherein an incoming heel or babyface was given options for certain apartment complexes into which they could move. And they were also given the names of the complexes they were to avoid.

In the arenas, heels and faces dressed separately. Out of the arenas in Florida, heels and faces lived separately. Simple enough.

"In Tampa," Sullivan began, "everyone, kids included, were in a bubble." When Ben and Shannon came home from school everyday, their playmates were inhabitants of that same bubble. The Sullivan kids didn't spend much time deflecting comments about their dad's evil deeds because the kids playing with them in their apartment complex didn't have many questions about it.

What was Dutch Mantell's kid going to ask?

Or Steve Kiern's, for that matter?

Or Les Thornton's?

The Sullivan kids came home and bounced around the complex with the Mantell, Kiern, and Thornton kids, even the

Graham kids—promoter Eddie's grandkids, for a while. The kids were all under that same umbrella.

Tampa was popping and as new complexes were built, more and more attention had to be paid to who was living in which. Sullivan or Thornton, leaving their complex and moving into that new one down I-275, had better make sure no one working on the other side of the heel/face line had signed up for a unit in there as well.

The transient nature of the workers in the territory days of the sport precluded them from buying a house when moving into a new company. All of the guys got apartments.

When the first wrestler would move into one of the many new complexes in the city, the identity of that development was set—black hat or white hat. All of the wrestlers living in the city would not inhabit just two complexes. There might have been four guys in one development, five guys in another, maybe six or seven in still another. They were spread around a bit but rest assured, in Eddie Graham's territory, the babyfaces were living amongst each other. Same went for the bad guys.

The wives all got to know each other in the complex. They all worked to keep it a closed world, in a business where their husbands were working overtime to be hated by the general public.

The life of a child is the only life the child knows.

It seems elementary but it's a powerful statement and one we all wrestle with as parents. Growing up in the lap of luxury, in a home dripping with amenities, will set a certain standard of norms for a kid. A rigid, blue-collar home with dirty fingernails at the dinner table fosters yet another expectation. Some pretty desperate conditions for less fortunate children often yields a cycle of abuse, of self or others. In some cases it yields a flight from such conditions to great heights.

In all cases, they know only what they've lived.

Though not without its sacrifices, as we've seen, it must have been great fun to be the child of a pro wrestler in an age where they were regarded as superheroes. Tito took the kids on the road to local stops in the Northeast, and Bischoff's kids hit Disney for the TV tapings. We've heard that some kids were indifferent to it all, but a dad with a black "X" on his forehead raising The Purple Haze from the sea is a lot cooler than dad the electrician.

The school years lay the foundational elements, social and otherwise, in the child's life. They're working it out in the schoolyard, managing their time with homework, and dealing with conflict. Other kids become aware of family situations and they're ready to pounce or praise.

His parents are divorced.

Her dad is on TV.

His dad has a plane.

Wrestlers' kids seemed to have a handle on things. In no case did we see any torment at the hands of classmates. Sullivan's kids were in the enclave of Tampa apartment buildings, surrounded by other kids of wrestlers. Russo kept the kids away from any aspect of the business altogether. Bischoff and Gary Hart had their kids very close to the business and they saw it operate from the inside.

Flipping through all of our profiled examples shows a diversity in the ways their kids interacted with the business, and to what degree. And in most cases there was equilibrium.

Shane Bigelow struggled with the drug addiction of his father, which was brought about by Bam Bam's need to fight chronic pain. In the broadest sense, the wresting business brought Shane great strain and, ultimately, estrangement from his father. Tony Atlas and his daughter were estranged as well, and that was done at the hands of the wrestling business's travel requirements. Their relationships with their dads may have gone much differently if they weren't pro wrestlers.

Outside of those two, our profiled children knew how to file wrestling in their lives—either as fans who embraced it, or kids who were indifferent to it. Dad was just dad. Didn't really matter what he did for work.

5.

GOING HOME

AFTER THE RING, the pro wrestler finds himself not having to race from city to city, managing a couple of hundred dates each year. There was no retirement plan and with few exceptions, when the wrestling world was done with him, that was it. The era of which we speak offered no opportunity for producer positions, no trainer jobs in developmental federations.

Home. How unfamiliar. The kids are around, and older. There's the wife. And there he is.

What's next?

The answer ranges and if he made it out the other side with his health, sanity, and family in tact, the next quarter century could certainly challenge all that. The business goes on, evolves. Eventually he won't recognize it. But for now, outside of being recognized at the grocery store, he's on the outside of wrestling.

What shape one ends up in after wrestling depends greatly on how they handled their years in the wrestling business. If the worker's family has been damaged by their time on the road, then there is some fence mending to do now. The marriage may or may not have survived, as we've seen in our pithy study. The kids are grown and it may be time for reconciliation or even familiarization.

Pro wrestling was a passion for these performers. That's a crucial thing to bear in mind when considering the retired wrestler's return home. It was likely not a celebrated milestone. It was the death of the wrestler's first love. It was the death of a dream.

Unless the worker was incredibly disciplined and wise with money, it's also the death of a significant and steady income. With the wrestler on the road for 300 dates a year, the wife was probably not working. The loss of wrestling from the home was sometimes a great burden. The "real world" skill set of a wrestler of the 70s and 80s was anemic in some cases. It added to the emotional turmoil of leaving the business.

Whatever the familial circumstances to which the worker returns home, they will probably be doing so depressed, a huge part of them now amputated.

SHANE:
Bam Bam's bike

THERE WAS A GUY standing in front of Shane Bigelow asking him if he'd like to buy a particular motorcycle. Shane knew the bike. He hadn't seen it in quite a while, but he knew it. It was the real deal.

It was once Bam Bam's motorcycle. And now, thanks to the random man before him, for a few grand Shane could have his dad's old bike.

It's not an offer to buy back a long-lost token, though. There's no nostalgia in this, no glorious recouping of his dad's old prize. Actually, the bike is no longer a memory that Shane wants around, let alone the actual vehicle. In fact, everything about Bam Bam's last years on earth are memories that are better left elsewhere. Maybe in this fan's garage, beside the motorcycle.

As bad as Bam Bam's decline was for Shane and everyone

191

else, his overdose death in January 2007 was a mess. Shane didn't talk to his father for a year and a half before his passing, with the exception of a couple of short phone calls. They hadn't gone their separate ways over a big blowout. There was no final straw, no concluding fight. But the time he spent living with his father flipped a switch in Shane.

Bam Bam had become something that Shane hated. He hated to watch it, he hated being around it. He hated admitting that someone he was so proud of, so proud to call his father, had become someone so unlike himself. Shane was angry.

Bam Bam moved west to Pennsylvania in a section appropriately called Hideaway. That was the point where Shane lost contact with him. Shane was 17 years-old and didn't understand the totality of what was happening. The draw of addiction and its relationship to the constant physical pain Bam Bam was in didn't register with him.

Shane was still a kid, and he'd been betrayed by the image of the larger than life dad who made him feel so loved. That powerful, living legend was indestructible. His father being complicit in the undoing of that cloak of safety and security was unforgivable. Bam Bam wasn't only killing himself.

After some time of not speaking to his dad, Shane began college. On his first day back after winter break, he got a strange, random phone call on his cell. It was his tattoo guy, who never called to shoot the shit.

"Hey man," the guy said. "Are you alright?" As out of place as that was from this source, at once Shane knew this was the call he'd been expecting for the past year and a half.

As the details surrounding the death of his father emerged, Shane couldn't ignore some of the curious circumstances that were unearthed. Bam Bam had moved out of Hideaway, Pennsylvania and to the Tampa area. He got down there and moved in with an uncle who, in Shane's search for answers regarding the death, left more questions than answers.

When police entered the apartment and found Bam Bam's body, they took note of the dresser drawers having been ransacked. Bam Bam's jewelry was gone from his jewelry box as well. It was noteworthy enough for authorities to report back to the Bigelow family.

How suspicious were these findings, really? The nature of an addict's overdose death creates some stock answers to those kinds of things in an investigator's mind. Are ransacked drawers really that unusual for a junkie on a binge?

Where the hell are those few bucks I had?

I need those damn pills I stashed right now...where the fuck are they?

Those kind of crime scenes are not as cut and dry. There was no doubt that Bam Bam had been hocking his possessions for the few years prior to his death. That could have easily explained any jewelry he'd accumulated over the years being absent from the apartment. By that point, Shane was simply too far removed from his father's life to know for sure what added up and what didn't.

Then there was the matter of the toxicology. Bam Bam had so many drugs in his system when he died that it raised questions as to whether or not he could have been conscious long enough to ingest that much. As it was put to Shane, most normal people would have passed out before finishing a stash like that. But realistically, how can you validate an addict's tolerance for drugs, especially after his having built up such a resistance over the years? Who's to say that the average person's limitation for consumption was also the case for Bam Bam?

Suppose it was beyond the realm of possibility that Bigelow sat and consumed that much on his own. The big question is if Bam Bam *didn't* take them voluntarily, who gave them to him? And why? And why that much?

In one of the brief phone calls they had near the end, Bam Bam told Shane that he was due a pretty big royalty check in 2007 from a new licensing deal for a Bam Bam Bigelow toy action figure. With his finances in shambles, this was to be a life saver for him. He spoke about it a lot. He was looking forward to that check—a long overdue testament to his contributions to the business. But more than that, some much needed breathing room in his bank account.

He wouldn't live to see it. But, ostensibly, Bam Bam's kids would.

But when they didn't, they looked into just why that was. They contacted the company and learned the check was cut by the company and mailed to the proper address. It was soon discovered that the uncle with whom Bam Bam was rooming had cashed Bam Bam's $84,000 royalty check by using the kids' names. This discovery did nothing to quell Shane's persistent questions about that living situation as it related to the addiction, the quantity of drugs in Bam Bam's system, missing jewelry, and the death itself.

It would take nine years to navigate the red tape and legalities of getting a replacement check. By the time they did, Bam Bam's lingering medical bills had swelled to a $60,000 debt. In the end, Bam Bam's three children split a $24,000 inheritance—the remainder of the $84,000 check, after Bam Bam's debts were satisfied.

All of Bam Bam's years in rings for all federations, Wrestlemanias, pay-per-view buys, big houses overseas—all reduced to $24,000. Split three ways.

These days people still come up to Shane and tell him they bought items from Bam Bam that he was hocking when down and out. They offer to sell it back to Shane as if it were a favor. Imagine paying a few grand for a constant reminder of your father's demise? Shane makes his feelings about such a proposition clear to the man offering his dad's motorcycle.

"Fuck you, dude."

Shane's younger brother threw himself into amateur wrestling to escape the pain of Bam Bam's death. He was once an outgoing spirit, a very lively kid. Since Bam Bam's demise, he's become withdrawn. He was crushed, and justifiably so. Their little sister was too young to remember anything significant.

When they are all together with their mom now, the Bigelow kids share only laughs when talking about their father. Mom always tried to emphasize the good times and keep the memories positive. Bam Bam Bigelow had a significant, positive impact on his family before things went dark. Shane's mantra, "Don't half-ass it—commit fully," is still said in his father's voice. He can hear him say it. It was a lifelong gift.

When they are all together and a memory pops up and has the three of them laughing, it's clear there are still positive gifts for all of them. Bam Bam gave them more than enough to keep his legacy shining.

When they go down memory lane, it's all life before the pills.

LANNY:
Closer than ever

JUDY POFFO WAS looking at a beautiful baby. Though not necessarily her nature to lavish one with compliments, she must have been thinking that through it all, her son Lanny did a great job with Magen. The baby she was watching was, in fact, Magen's son.

At age 90, Judy became a great-grandmother. With his mom in failing health, Lanny relied on Apple's Facetime feature to bring his new baby grandson to his mom's eyes. It brought a smile to her face in her waning days. That was something Lanny tried for a lifetime and couldn't do himself, but the baby did. And Lanny held the iPhone for her when it did.

Magen and Lanny are closer than ever. Through his absences due to WWE's road demands and the divorce from Sally, they never drifted. He always had time for her and he never had a problem driving to Sarasota to see her.

"We never left each other," he says. Nowadays, they bond over health foods. The two health nuts share readings and findings with each other.

In raising Magen, Lanny always erred on the side of kindness. He wouldn't escalate situations. Lanny gravitated to a side of the world apart from his brother Randy, who was loaded with aggression. About the worst Lanny could be accused of was being more of a friend than an authority figure to Magen as she got older.

Lanny and his grandson

From Lanny's perspective it's clear that he attributes the greatest contribution to the success of his relationship with

Magen and her development into a strong, independent woman is his example of clean living. Okay, he shot some steroids in the late 80s, but through it all he saw that as occupational hazard. It was a short period and workers around him were taking excess to new levels. With so many stories in wrestling having such dark overtones, he feels that clean living would have given troubled workers the best chance at succeeding as fathers.

"We were never closer than we are now," he said of Magen.

Though Lanny and Magen needed no time for resolution after Lanny left the ring, there was emotional restitution to be made elsewhere.

Toward the end of Angelo's life, as his health was in decline, Lanny would pick him up every Sunday and drive him to the nearby Catholic church. He felt Angelo, staring at the blackness and uncertainty of eternity, deserved that peace of mind. However, Lanny certainly hadn't yet found anything comforting about the religion Angelo chose for himself and Lanny as well.

But these trips were for his father. They were a gesture for the man who cast a long shadow over Lanny's life. It was a silent commentary that replaced any of those late-in-life, reflective discussions that no Poffo was going to have. After Lanny's struggle for independence, his insistence on bucking Angelo's influence on his parenting Magen, and his being pinned between a triad of dictators in the Poffo home, he drove that man to find a peace as his exit neared. Lanny, ever steadfast in his view of the bigger picture, would do that for the final act of the patriarch's time here.

"Even as I was doing that," Lanny began, "I said to myself, 'The minute I don't have to do this anymore, the next time I'm in a Catholic church I'll be horizontal.'"

The words "have to do this" may be the most telling commentary of all.

Angelo Poffo died on March 4, 2010 at 84 years-old.

JJ:
We all survived

THROUGH ALL THE ups and downs, JJ Dillon's first wife, Lynda, remains the one that will probably show up at the first sign of need. 52 years after their marriage, they speak and maintain a great friendship to this day. She's nearby to Delaware resident JJ, in Reading, Pennsylvania, as is their daughter Pam. JJ sees Pam and his four granddaughters and they talk frequently.

JJ's wild ride is pulling into the station now. At 75 years of age, JJ lives with Amanda and Geoffrey, his twins, both 25 years-old. Amanda is working in the medical field and Geoffrey is pretty independent, using a motorized wheelchair to get around. Cooking is a challenge, as his strength is compromised on his left side, so JJ still has to assist with that due to the danger of potential burns. But outside of that, Geoffrey can pretty much do it all.

JJ doesn't speak with their mother, his third wife Lindsey. Their last child remains quite close to mom.

He hasn't seen his second wife, Jeanette, since the divorce either. At 80 years old, she still lives in Charlotte. JJ also doesn't keep in touch with his 3 stepsons from that marriage.

JJ's two step nieces, whom he and Jeanette took in after the tragic overdose death of their mother, are still on his radar though. One lives in Oregon, and the second spent some time in California and recently moved to Connecticut. After not seeing them for all those years, he stopped in on his way to Massachusetts. They still refer to him as their "second father."

What he and Jeanette did for the girls was heroic. The ramifications of a mess like the overdose death could have been so destructive. It is not without its residue, even now. But the stability JJ and Jeanette provided gave them something tangible to hold onto through that agonizing time.

"You do something at the time, you don't think anything of it," JJ says of the decision to raise them. "I was in the business and doing well and was able to do for them. It was just something where they didn't have anyone else and I was here. I didn't think of it as a big deal or do it for pats on the back."

Looking back, one has to wonder how much of the diversity of JJ's familial journey is a result of being in the topsy-turvy wrestling world. Unpredictability comes with the territory in wrestling, so one has to have a tolerance for it, or perhaps an attraction to it. Then there are the household challenges a wrestler's schedule adds, which we've explored throughout this study. Would JJ have had the same success/failure rate with marriage if he were a CEO or postal worker? The truth, JJ says, is somewhere in the middle.

"The wrestling world does not make it easy to have a traditional marriage, family, or household which you'd call a *normal* household," he says. "But we all seem to have survived."

TONY:
I thought you were dead

IN 2005, A YOUNG, black man came up to Tony Atlas in the Bahamas. He introduced himself and then blew Tony's mind.

"Tony," he said, "I live across the street from your daughter." Tony had been trying to make contact with her for many years and this guy seemed to have dropped from the sky. Tony's life had become a roller coaster after his mainstream run in WWE, then a brief and ridiculous return to the WWE rings as Saba Simba. Tony Atlas, the bodybuilding champion known as "Mr. USA" for his major wrestling runs, was then expected to convince audiences that he was an African warrior. This was less than ten years after his "Mr. USA" run.

In the midst of that, Tony became a lost soul, eventually becoming homeless and living in a park. Tony detailed digging himself into burrows under park benches to stay dry when sleeping. He was very much off the grid.

Imagine his ex-wife Joyce's surprise when the young man returned from the Bahamas and delivered to her and Nikki Tony's contact info.

"I thought you were dead," Joyce said into the phone. She and Tony hadn't spoken in 25 years, and he hadn't seen their daughter Nikki since she was 11 years-old. They would occasionally talk on the phone, but he didn't see her in her teenage years or beyond.

Then came the phone call when she told Tony she was pregnant.

"I didn't like it," Tony says. "She told me she was getting married and I didn't like it. I never got good news when she'd call."

Tony's distaste for the pregnancy and marriage likely comes from the profile of his son-in-law—he's only six years younger than Tony. Tony feels that his absence created the void that she filled with this man considerably older than she.

"Most girls that don't have a father are attracted to older men, to replace him. So she married him to replace me." The man treats Nikki well, from what Tony knows. That should usurp any criticism, but when Tony considers that replacement, he likely feels a sense of guilt.

Once Joyce found him, it would be time to see where he and Nikki were at. Discussions between the father and daughter were strained and reconciliation didn't seem possible. "She was told stuff by her mom," Tony says. Nikki would not accept that Tony loved her. From her perspective, and perhaps some dots connected by Joyce, her father left her. That left a significant scar and she holds significant resentment.

"She don't wanna hear it. If I told her the story, she would just hang up the phone. She don't wanna hear that." From Tony's point of view, Joyce made the choice to head back to Alabama and before Tony knew it, there were divorce papers being sent to him with the threat of having him locked up if he didn't sign them. They'd force court appearances on him and when he missed any due to the Mid-Atlantic road schedule, he'd have a *failure to appear*. "I never got the chance to explain to Nikki what really happened."

The kind of sporadic phone contact he had with her over the years was not the kind Tony wanted. "The only time my daughter called me was when she wanted money," he says. "No other time."

In 2009, Tony was called back to WWE and paired as Mark Henry's manager. Tony did the full road schedule and hit cities all across the county. When he was near Nikki in Alabama, she'd come to the matches. Even today he tries to get indie bookings near her and his grandchildren. "Whenever I'm in the area, I'll stop by and see her. Last time I cut the grass."

Tony's wrestling dreams are done. He had great runs, and then runs where he felt that Vince McMahon and WWE were erecting his tombstone by making him a flunkey for a contemporary superstar. He has one dream today. It's farfetched, but simple.

"Hit the lottery so I can set them up, and my grandkids, and spend more time with them. I want to do for my grandkids what I was not able to do for my daughter."

The drive behind his dream is as simple as it is heartbreaking.

"I feel like if I can do for my grandkids, my daughter will start to love me again."

SEAN:
Uncle Gary

THOUGH CERTAINLY not a member of Gary Hart's family, I will be handling this chapter myself. The reason being, I was a part of the finish of Gary Hart's story.

As an owner of the professional wrestling production company Kayfabe Commentaries, I had occasion to hire Gary for a spot on our popular series *Guest Booker*. The show profiles actual bookers of the sport and challenges them with a booking exercise wherein we watch their process in real time. We felt it was an important and unique show for the sport.

We'd produced four episodes of the series up to that time— ones with Kevin Sullivan, JJ Dillon, Gabe Sapolsky, and Raven. When we were offered Gary as a potential guest for the series, we jumped at the opportunity. I was a fan of Gary's as a heel manager, but I also knew he was integral to the Dallas wrestling territory, serving as its booker during some of its more successful years.

On March 14, 2008, Gary flew out to Pennsylvania where we set up for what would become a historic edition—not simply for its great content, but because it was the last thing in which Gary Hart ever appeared.

Gary came out to Nowhere, Pennsylvania and knocked out *Guest Booker #5,* charming us the entire time with his wisdom and sense of humor. We shared a cocktail and shot a great edition of the series.

After we wrapped, Gary stayed and sat around the set while we broke down the large hotel suite. There was a UFC show on that night and Gary and the KC guys talked the sport, of which I had little interest. But the vibe was like we all knew each other. He mentioned his sons back home in Texas and took the time to foster a real bond. Some cats take the envelope, sing the song, and head out the stage door. And that's fine. It's whey we are there.

But that night it was the KC guys and Uncle Gary.

We left Pennsylvania talking not about how good the show was, or if the booking exercise was realistic—but rather how cool Gary was. To this date I don't think any talent has ever won us over like he did.

On Sunday morning, I awoke to a full Blackberry. It didn't give me a chance to ignore it until after breakfast, which was my plan. And seeing the subject line in James Soubasis of Legends of the Ring's text ensured that.

Did Gary Hart die?

God. Hope not. Seemed fine when we were together.

Then, agent Eric Simms called and confirmed the grim news. I was shocked. Gary had made all his shots up here in the Northeast and flown home. When his son Jason tried to get in touch with him, they'd had plans to meet up on Sunday and watch a couple of the NBA games, he couldn't get him. It was soon discovered that Gary was dead of a heart attack.

I was pretty hard hit, not just because I'd worked with him. I've worked with people that died. I just had this bizarre feeling that it wasn't his time yet. It was ridiculous—I'd known him for six hours. There's no rational justification for feeling that way or *any* way about someone I barely knew. For all I knew, he could have just really enjoyed talking about booking Texas, loved our show, enjoyed our charming crew, and then went back to his life as an axe murderer.

But I really didn't think so. Gary was one of those guys into whose eyes you could look and see his soul. He meant the things he said when he was going over the booking of Texas with us, but he wasn't boisterous or showy. He was the soft-spoken professor, but his advantage over the guys in the sport jackets on campus was that Gary lived it.

And he was gone, just like that. I spent that day fielding calls about his time with us, his final hours on the planet. There was really nothing to report. He was fine. Watch the episode of *Guest Booker*, you'll see. But the wrestling media was all over this and our name kept coming up as the last production company with which he worked, and by a matter of hours.

The following day, I answered a call from his son Jason. I

will never forget how ripped apart his voice was. That was probably the hardest phone call the guy ever had to make, and I was aware of that when I spoke to him. He knew that his dad was slated to appear on *Guest Booker* and he'd read in the press coverage of his death that we'd shot it on Friday night.

Jason was trying to piece together the final days of his father's life. The death was so sudden, Jason must've needed something more concrete to grasp than, "He was here, now he's not." We don't function well that way. We need to make a mental and spiritual transition from one's being alive to their being gone. When there are multiple dogs in a home, one's death is only understood by the others if they see the body, sniff the lifeless dog. Otherwise it's just expected they will return.

I was at a funeral once and was taking a breather down in one of the lounges near the restrooms. There was a small, unassuming poster on the wall. It was letter-sized, framed in glass, just words. It was called "What is a Funeral?"

That was a great question. I'd pondered the perverse ritual of staring at the corpse of a loved one almost every time I attended one. I'd buried my father, all grandparents, uncles, a young cousin, and just too many people by the time I was 30.

Why do we all have to get together and stare at that coffin—that caricature of the undead and vampires and shit? Look around—everyone's crying, miserable. What is this thing?

And that little article I saw on the wall was so succinct, and it all instantly made sense. The funeral is that bridge we must mentally build, like the dead dog we have to show to the living ones before they can move on. It closes a door on someone for us. We continue to grieve and ache, but we are at an understanding with this from a subconscious sense.

I was that door for Jason. He'd talked to dad, he was going to Pennsylvania to shoot a show and meet some fans at a signing, and then he was gone. *What the hell?*

Jason wanted to know if I saw anything amiss with Gary—confusion, pain. I didn't. He was great, I told him. I couldn't be that bridge for Jason, but he knew I had that footage of his dad, more recent than Jason had laid eyes on him. I assured Jason that I wanted his family's input on the show. I didn't want him to think we would be opportunistic about his dad's passing, in regards to the release of the show. I wanted to take some time. I wanted to do it right.

I asked Jason for photos of Gary with him and his brother, Chad. You've seen them in this book, and we also ran the end credits of *Guest Booker with Gary Hart* over them. We cut a trailer in advance of the release date—a music video with shots from the show and also those personal pictures, which we subtitled "Gary Goes Home." We played the track "Hands of Time" by Groove Armada. It was quite nice. Search it out on YouTube, it's still there.

Ultimately, Jason said his family trusted me and left the details of the show's release in our hands—from the timing to the advertising. When Jason first saw the advance trailer with the photos Gary, him, and Chad, he called me to thank me. But not for the obvious reasons.

"I'm so relieved you handled the music like you did," he said. "I was so scared you'd play some Celine Dion shit for my dad."

VINCE:
The Internet

THE VINCE RUSSO Hate Club made their unofficial home online in the late 90s and up through his tenure at TNA Wrestling later on. His kids were spared most of the vitriol directed at their father due to their having been too young to browse the Internet. Because they weren't fans of wrestling, they weren't seeing what he was doing on-camera either. For the first half of their lives, they knew their dad did something with wrestling, and that thing kept him away a lot.

Vince kept them from the business and, except for very rare occasions, that was fine with them. Seemed to work out for everyone. Will, V.J., and Annie weren't privy to the negativity surrounding Russo. And there was a lot of it. Once Russo got to WCW, he invited some that heat as well by becoming a bad guy on-camera. There was already plenty of scuttlebutt by

Internet wrestling fans who knew Russo and his partner Ferrara had jumped ship, and were now in charge of the WCW product.

Russo played to the negative vibes aimed at him, admitting he took every part of his brash, Northeast cockiness and amplified it by 10, sensing fans of the WCW product didn't need much convincing to hate New York bravado. Internet fans continued to bash him for questionable creative decisions as head writer, and now fans in arenas booed him. Through it all, he managed to keep his family happily oblivious to all of it.

Today Russo's kids are grown, on their own, and carry their own Intent connected devices. In a delayed reaction, today they see scathing things written about their dad—some old, some current. Yes, he still ruffles feathers today.

But now, Will calls him and asks him about what he's reading. Russo doesn't so much mind what he reads about himself. His kids are a different story.

"Everything everyone says about me now, my kids read," he begins. "When you're labeling their father a racist, and a sexist, and a homophobe—these are my kids that have been with me my whole, entire life and they know me inside and out and who my friends are and who I hung out with—and they hear shit like that, and that's what people don't think about."

If he were given the gift of hindsight, one small change could have fixed the stresses of the past 25 years. Tweaking one detail would have given him his kids back and allowed him to see them through their most formative years.

"I would have not gotten in the business," Russo says. "Looking back now, I would have given everything to have gotten another job."

For Vince Russo, wrestling has taken much more from him than it gave.

ERIC:
Thank you

IT WAS 2007 AND Eric Bischoff stood poised in his tuxedo, listening for his cue. The music would play and he walk out, down the aisle, past the people and their cameras. He was already smiling and his trademark, china-white pearlies would stay out for the people. This was a big entrance, a huge honor. It put a different sort of butterfly in his belly than wrestling did.

But wrestling was so good to him and his family, and the view he was able to give them from atop WCW contributed greatly to their success. As of this writing, Montanna is an executive in TV production for Time Warner. She lives in Marina del Rey, doing great—her success, no doubt, sprouted from seeds of creativity planted in and around her life in her formative years.

She sees TV production in her earliest memories, not from a

class trip or *Sesame Street* segment. Rather, from being
ensconced in it and watching her father navigate its choppy and
temperamental tide. Talent is a hassle. Production schedules
and release dates are as well, at any level of that art. Montanna
watched it, and then landed in it.

Garett took a more direct route, ending up in TNA
Wrestling with Eric for a few years. Talent aside, Garett's
greatest asset, one most rare for a young wrestler starting out,
was his years of exposure to the psychology of the sport. Garett
could easily skip that chapter of the newbie handbook—he'd
lived with its author and his friends. He was able to walk into
TNA perhaps lacking the physical familiarity with a canvass
mat, but with years of insight into the magic that makes people
scream, cheer, and pay.

"If I ever won the Powerball and had more money than I knew what to do with, and I wanted to entertain myself and launch a wrestling company," Eric says, "Garett would be a very valuable asset, as a result of everything he's learned. Garett right now could do as good a job laying out a great match, with a great story, and probably come up with three or four great finishes, than anyone outside of WWE right now."

To the Bischoffs, wrestling gave. It took nothing, if not some time away from home while setting up the machine that would carry them into the sunset. But clearly, that time away was a small sacrifice for the experience that paid dividends.

"My kids had experiences with my wife and I that have changed their lives because of the business," he says. "They have friends in Japan to this day."

The Bischoff family was invited to Japan courtesy of New Japan Pro Wrestling. They flew first-class, stayed in the finest hotels and once Eric and Masa Saito finished their appointed business, they took a remarkable five days to see the country. They were shown rare and luxurious aspects of Japanese life by Saito and his wife. They took the bullet train to Hokkaido and participated in the ancient ritual of the mineral bath. The Bischoff family got into their robes, were served a formal dinner, and went out into the freezing mountains in January, to the hot springs among the ghosts of samurai past.

Thank you, Dad. Thank you, Verne.

"Wrestling diversified them and educated them in their view of the world in a way that you just can't get reading a book, seeing a movie, or taking a class," Eric said.

And there's the music—Eric's cue. He looked to his partner at his right and smiled. It was time. He could see out—the cameras went up, the video guy was in the aisle, ready to backtrack as they moved down the walkway.

It was hard to fight that lump in the throat, even for the hardened TV executive with the black belt. He stepped out with Amy on his arm. A decade or so after her mom requested she stay with the Bischoffs to escape the tumult of her home, she had a request of her own for Eric. She wanted him to give her away at her wedding.

And he did, in a moment unforgettable for him—a guy who got lots of chances, and her—a young lady who was given one big one.

Thank you, wrestling.

ABOUT THE AUTHOR

Sean Oliver is the author of the Kindle #1 Bestseller *Kayfabe*, which documents his time as co-owner of Kayfabe Commentaries, a wrestling-oriented production company.

Sean's first novel, *Sophie's Journal,* a psychological thriller, was released in 2018. He has also worked in film and television for 25 years with over a hundred credits on major motion pictures and television series.

Sean lives in New Jersey with his wife and two daughters, none of them wrestlers.

FOLLOW SEAN

Keep tabs on what he has going on in the world of both fiction and non-fiction.

WEBSITE:

http://seanoliverbooks.com/

BOOKBUB:

https://www.bookbub.com/authors/sean-oliver

AMAZON AUTHOR CENTRAL:

https://www.amazon.com/Sean-Oliver/e/B077P8Q8TX

TWITTER:

https://twitter.com/kayfabesean

GET YOUR COPY OF SEAN'S KINDLE #1 BESTSELLER, *KAYFABE,* TODAY

"Look, let me make this as simple as possible-for 25 years I worked in a business full of liars, cheaters, workers, con artists and of course, politicians. I can name maybe 3 people over the years that I 100% trusted-or-even <u>believed</u> for that matter. Sean Oliver is one of those men. In reading Kayfabe *you can believe that 100% of this masterpiece is accurate-yes-even the parts about me. The most stand-up guy perhaps ever associated with the business of professional wrestling. You want truth-you'll find it right here. BRAVO!"*

- Vince Russo, Former WWE/WCW Head Writer

www.SeanOliverBooks.com

Made in the USA
Monee, IL
26 May 2022

97087914R00134